FOOD FOR THOUGHT

BEING A COMPENDIUM OF CULINARY QUIPS, QUOTES, ANECDOTES, FACTS, & RECIPES BY THE GREAT AND NOT-SO-GREAT

COMPILED AND EDITED BY IAN MAKAY

The Crossing Press
Freedom, CA 95019

This book is dedicated with all my love to
Bernadette and Alexander.

To the many beautiful and wonderful things
we have created and shared and will create
and share both inside and outside the
kitchen.

Copyright © 1995 by Bay Publishing
Book Design by Sheryl Karas

Printed in the U.S.A.

Library of Congress Cataloging-in-Publication Data

Food For Thought : being a compendium of culinary quips, quotes, anecdotes, facts & recipes by the great and not-so-great / compiled and edited by Ian Makay.
     p. cm.
  Includes indexes.
  ISBN 0-89594-762-5 (paper)
  1. Food—Quotations, maxims, etc. 2. Food—Miscellanea.
I. Makay, Ian.
PN6084.F6F65 1995
641—dc20
                                       95-20214
                                       CIP

ACKNOWLEDGEMENTS

Although, typically, the person whose name appears on the cover of a book gets the credit (or the blame) for it, books are the fruit of many people's hard work, creativity, and inspiration. In no particular order, here are those who, obviously or not, made this book possible.

My thanks to the good people at The Crossing Press—especially Dennis Hayes—who have truly made creating this book more of a love than a labor for me. It is their artistic, marketing, and managerial creativity that has put the book you see into your hands.

A word of gratitude to all the other editors and publishers who seriously looked at the proposal for this book, but passed on it. Your feedback and encouragement along the way attests to the fact that this business has a heart and soul as well as a bottom line.

To my original family—my mother and my father, my grandparents, and the interesting assortment of aunts, uncles, and cousins—who fed my sister and me food and love and in the process fostered my passion for both, there are no words to adequately express my debt or gratitude. How lucky I am to have been born into a family and raised in a culture that intertwines food and love in a positive way. It has engendered my recognition of the value of fellowship that comes with breaking bread together. It acknowledges the contributions of both host and guest, of the souls that create the feast and the good hearts that relish sharing it.

To the family added to the table—Bernadette, my wife, Alexander, my son, and the many friends—my thanks and love for choosing to give me your special gift. You have cooked and eaten good food with me and nourished me with your company.

To the many chefs, hosts, waiters, busboys, dishwashers and the hundred hidden others who have entertained, educated, and enriched my life with their talents and hard work, thank you for doing so. As I have wandered through what sometimes has seemed an endless maze of eateries, cookbooks, and cooking shows, three individuals have inspired me, above all others, by making food and cooking accessible and fun. Through their warmth, sincerity, and humor, Julia Child, Graham Kerr, and Jeff Smith have added more to my appreciation of and attitude about cooking and eating than they will ever fully comprehend.

Finally, and I know this isn't a football game or the Academy Awards, I want to thank the Creator. However you envision that being to be, let us always be thankful to the Creator for the rich table that is spread before us and for the many blessings that we have and constantly continue to receive.

LE MENU DU JOUR

Food has been a passion, a magnificent obsession, of mine since early childhood. Vivid memories of eating Teta Maria's homemade gnocchi while watching the cartoon version of *Gulliver's Travels* on my fourth birthday leap into view with the mere scent of shalsa. Details of the room, the lighting, the company, the movie, the aromas, the visceral pleasure of chewing on each dumpling, are all clear—each image emanating from the steaming bowl in front of me as if it, through every strand of heat wafting through the room, were the conductor of some magical symphony that was my birthday.

Words have also been an integral part of who I am, although the reasons for this would require much more explanation than there is room to accommodate here. (We might also need a couch and a therapist to fully delve into that one.) Quotes, those compact philosophical gems, whether profound, humorous, revealing, or just entertaining, have been especially intriguing to me and I have, over time, become an ardent compiler of them.

It had occurred to me some time ago combining these two interests of mine into a book or books would be a great idea in itself. Food, in its myriad forms, has been made into a natural metaphor for life time and again by gastronomes, philosophers, writers, kings, queens, celebrities, and other less notable contributors to the tomes of time. Food is life—a fact sometimes overlooked by those of us who spend more time worrying about what to eat and how to eat rather than if we *will* eat. But for the vast majority of the world's inhabitants, both currently and throughout recorded time, the relationship between food and staying alive has not gone unnoticed. As such, it conjures up thoughts, memories, and feelings closer to the soul of humanity than even the greatest writers, thinkers, and pundits could ever hope to come.

Religion and history provide a veritable smorgasbord of edible abstractions basted in myth and reality.

A humble apple, or some reasonably similar fruit substitute endemic to the Tigris and Euphrates valleys, caused humanity's downfall in the Garden of Eden. (Granted, Adam and Eve probably played some minor role too.) Manna, bread from heaven, miraculously sustained the Hebrews as they wandered in the desert. The magical powers of coffee were revealed to a lowly young goatherder through his flock—an instrument of Allah—a gift to the faithful. The last straw igniting the American Revolution and with it a revolutionary political philosophy was tea, while references to what pastries the French peasants should eat caused other leaders to lose their heads in a more literal sense.

This brief sampling of epicurean delights gives us reason enough to question whether Freud was misdirected in his theories—perhaps it isn't the figure mom cuts, per se, but her cookie cutter that has driven countless of us to the therapist's couch. Was Descartes misquoted? While there remains some question about how deeply, if at all, we each think (look at politicians, for example), we all must nourish ourselves physically. Ergo, what Descartes must have truly said was, "I eat, therefore I am." Therein lies an indisputable fact.

Thankfully, or so you may think by this juncture, *Food for Thought* relies primarily on the insight and observations of others rather than on my own. Organized as a menu of quotes, anecdotes, food facts, and *unusual* recipes of one kind or another culled from the cookbooks of history, this compendium serves not as the last word on food and things related, but as a beginning for pondering and wondering, remembering and relishing the value of food in all its many forms throughout your own life.

There is nothing left to add but *bon appétit!*

January 1995
Ian Makay

A Word to Our Patrons

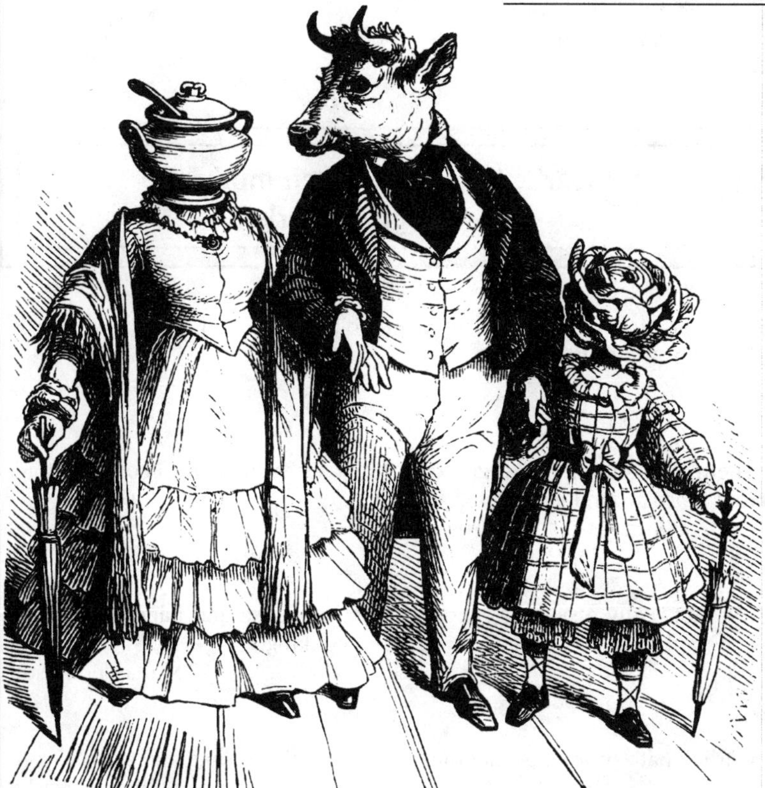

Tomatoes and oregano make it Italian; wine and tarragon make it French. Sour cream makes it Russian; lemon and cinnamon make it Greek. Soy sauce makes it Chinese; garlic makes it good.

—Alice May Brock

There is no such thing as a little garlic.

—Arthur Baer

> # Garlic is as good as ten mothers.
> ## —Telugu Proverb

There are many miracles in the world to be celebrated and, for me, garlic is the most deserving.

—Leo Buscaglia

There's something about garlic that creates excitement. People can get real loose around garlic.

—Lloyd Harris

It is not really an exaggeration to say that peace and happiness begin, geographically, where garlic is used in cooking.

—X. Marcel Boulestin

Garlick hath properties that make a man winke, drinke and stinke.

—Thomas Nashe

2

A nickel will get you on the subway, but garlic will get you a seat.
—New York Yiddish Proverb

In the beginning there was James Beard and there was curry and that was about all.
—Nora Ephron

I believe that if I ever had to practice cannibalism, I might manage if there was enough tarragon around.
—James Beard

In medieval times the habit arose of expressing a man's wealth, no longer in terms of the amount of land in his estate, but of the amount of pepper in his pantry. One way of saying that a man was poor was to say that he lacked pepper. The wealthy kept large stores of pepper in their houses, and let it be known that it was there: it was a guarantee of solvency.
—Waverley Root

Pepper is small in quantity and great in virtue.
—Plato

For a gourmet wine is not a drink but a condiment, provided that your host has chosen correctly.
—Edouard de Pomiane

Condiments are like old friends—highly thought of, but often taken for granted.
—Marilyn Kaytor

Mayonnaise: One of the sauces which serve the French in place of a state religion.

—Ambrose Bierce

Mustard: Good only in Dijon. Ruins the stomach.

—Gustave Flaubert

The French approach to food is characteristic; they bring to their consideration of the table the same appreciation, respect, intelligence and lively interest that they have for other arts, for painting, for literature, and for the theatre. We foreigners living in France respect and appreciate this point of view but deplore their too strict observance of a tradition which will not admit the lightest deviation in a seasoning or the suppression of a single ingredient. Restrictions aroused our American ingenuity, we found combinations and replacements which pointed in new directions and created a fresh and absorbing interest in everything pertaining to the kitchen.

—Alice B. Toklas

On American food:
A plenitude of peanut butter and a dearth of hot mustard.

—Patrick Dean

Americans can eat garbage, provided you sprinkle it liberally with ketchup, mustard, chili sauce, tabasco sauce, cayenne pepper, or any other condiment which destroys the original flavor of the dish.

—Henry Miller

On Edmund McIlhenny's development of Tabasco sauce in post-Civil War Louisiana:
He chopped up peppers, mixed them with vinegar and Avery Island salt, put the mixture in wooden barrels to age and funneled the resulting sauce into secondhand cologne bottles.

—James Conaway

On average shelf life of Tabasco sauce:
You can tell how long a couple has been married by whether they are on their first, second or third bottle of Tabasco.

—Bruce R. Bye

Parsley—the jewel of herbs, both in the pot and on the plate.

—Albert Stockli

GARNISH

Garnishing of dishes has also a great deal to do with the appearance of a dinner-table, each dish garnished sufficiently to be in good taste without looking absurd.
—Hugo Ziemann, Steward of the White House, and Mrs. F.L. Gillette
The Original White House Cookbook: Contains Cooking, Toilet and Household Recipes, Menus, Dinner-giving, Table Etiquette, Care of the Sick, Health Suggestions, Facts Worth Knowing, etc. (1887)

A man taking basil from a woman will always love her.

—Sir Thomas More

Nyons, itself, sheltered from the *mistral* wind by the low hills of Les Baronnies, is home to the most delicious olive in France. Small, oval and black, its dry yet buttery flavour has an intensity and almost wine-like taste unequalled anywhere. And, of course, the oil produced from these olives is superb. No matter that the oil has collected prizes and accolades for a century, your tongue and your palate will tell you that this is a classic among olive oils. It's not just a liquid that you slurp over salads or mix with lemon juice or wine vinegar; it is also a food with flavour and consistency to be valued in its own right. One of my grandfathers swallowed a teaspoonful every day of his life.

—Geraldene Holt

To be a gourmet you must start early, as you must begin riding early to be a good horseman. You must live in France, your father and mother must have been a gourmet. Nothing in life must interest you but your stomach.

—Ludwig Bemelmans

I want a dish to taste good, rather than to have been seethed in pig's milk and served wrapped in a rhubarb leaf with grated thistle root.

—Kingsley Amis

There is no way that you can run a proper kitchen without having fresh stocks on hand. If you buy commercially prepared products you are generally getting little more than salt, and in a very expensive form.

—Jeff Smith (The Frugal Gourmet)

6

Some people's food always tastes better than others, even if they are cooking the same dish at the same dinner. Now I will tell you why—because one person has more life in them—more fire, more vitality, more guts—than others. A person without these things can never make food taste right, no matter what materials you give them, it is no use. Turn in the whole cow full of cream instead of milk, and all the fresh butter and ingredients in the world, and still that cooking will taste dull and flabby—just because they have nothing in themselves to give. You have got to throw feeling into cooking.

—Rosa Lewis

Love and eggs are best when they are fresh.
—Russian Proverb

It was obvious that the egg had come first. There was something dignified about a silent passive egg, whereas Aunt Irene found it difficult to envisage an angel bearing a hen—which despite its undoubted merits, was a foolish and largely intractable bird.

—Alice Thomas Ellis

Alas! my child, where is the Pen
That can do justice to the Hen?
Like Royalty, she goes her way,
Laying foundations every day,
Though not for public buildings, yet
For Custard, Cake, and Omelette.
No wonder, child, we prize the Hen,
Whose Egg is mightier than the Pen.

—Oliver Herford

For flavor, instant sex will never supercede the stuff you have to peel and cook.

—Quentin Crisp

When poets...write about food it is usually celebratory. Food as the thing-in-itself, but also the thoughtful preparation of meals, the serving of meals, meals communally shared: a sense of the sacred in the profane.

—Joyce Carol Oates

HOW TO GATHER AND CLARIFIE MAY-DEWE

When there has fallen no raine the night before, then with a cleane and large sponge, the next morning you may gather the same from sweet herbs, grasse, or corne. Straine your dewe, and expose it to the sunn in glasses covered with papers or parchment prickt full of holes. Straine it often, continuing in the sunne, which will require the best part of the summer.

—Sir Hugh Platt
*Delightes for Ladies, to Adorne
Their Persons, Tables, Closets, and
Distillatories, With Bewties, Banquets,
Perfumes, and Waters* (1600)

The onion is the truffle of the poor.

—Robert J. Courtine

There has always been a food processor in the kitchen. But once upon a time she was usually called the missus, or Mom.

—Sue Berkman

Canning gives the American family—especially in cities and factory towns—a kitchen garden where all good things grow, and where it is always harvest time. There are more tomatoes in a ten-cent can than could be bought in city markets for that sum when tomatoes are at their cheapest, and this is true of most other tinned foods. A regular Arabian Nights garden, where raspberries, apricots, olives and pineapples, are always ripe, grow side by side with peas, pumpkins, spinach; a garden with baked beans, wines and spaghetti bushes, and sauerkraut beds, and great cauldrons of hot soup.

—James H. Collins

In the childhood memories of every good cook, there's a large kitchen, a warm stove, a simmering pot and a mom.

—Barbara Costikyan

Some sensible person once remarked that you spend the whole of your life either in bed or in your shoes. Having done the best you can by the shoes and the bed, devote all the time and resources at your disposal to the building up of a fine kitchen. It will be, as it should be, the most comforting and comfortable room in the house.

—Elizabeth David

Such is life. It is no cleaner than a kitchen; it reeks of a kitchen; and if you mean to cook your dinner, you must expect to soil your hands; the real art is in getting them clean again, and therein lies the whole morality of our epoch.

—Honoré de Balzac

> *A good meal ought to begin with hunger.*
> *—French Proverb*

We owe so much to the fruitful meditation of our sages, but a sane view of life is, after all, elaborated mainly in the kitchen.

—Joseph Conrad

Once learnt, this business of cooking was to prove an ever growing burden. It scarcely bears thinking about, the time and labour that man and womankind has devoted to the preparation of dishes that are to melt and vanish in a moment like smoke or a dream, like a shadow, and as a post that hastes by, and the air closes behind them, afterwards no sign where they went is to be found.

—Rose Macaulay

On an everyday basis we don't use a huge variety of ingredients but a core of foods treated under a variety of conditions to create new dishes—which is why we can eat substantially better than animals.

—Robert Del Grande

You should be an epicure as to your work.

—Eugène Delacroix

The true cook is the perfect blend, the only perfect blend, of artist and philosopher. He knows his worth: he holds in his palm the happiness of mankind, the welfare of generations yet unborn.

—Norman Douglas

> They had a Cook with them who stood alone
>   For boiling chicken with marrowbone,
> Sharp flavouring-powder and a spice for savour.
>   He could distinguish London ale by flavour,
> And he could roast and seethe and broil and fry,
>   Make good thick soup and bake a tasty pie....
> And as for blancmange, he made it with the best.
>   —Geoffrey Chaucer

The French peasant cuisine is at the basis of the culinary art. By this I mean it is composed of honest elements that *la grande cuisine* only embellishes.

—Alexandre Dumaine

Formerly, people believed that the sugar cane alone yielded sugar; nowadays it is extracted from almost anything. It is the same with poetry. Let us draw it, no matter whence, for it lies everywhere, and in all things.

—Gustave Flaubert

Working in the kitchen is like playing in a football game:
It's a total team thing. If there's a weak link, it just won't work.

—Charles Palmer

If you can organize your kitchen, you can organize your life.

—Louis Parrish

The big black six-burner stove, wedged between an auxiliary corner sink and the refrigerator, which we painted black, is the reason, we sometimes tell each other, that we bought the house. There were many, many reasons, of course, but the compelling appeal of this generously proportioned stove, fueled by outdoor tanks of propane, is clearly evident as it sits stolidly, comfortably, on the terra-cotta tile floor. It seems to have been invented to turn out feasts for a gathered family.

—Evan Jones

And what a stove it was! Broad-bosomed, ample, vast like a huge fertile black mammal whose breasts would suckle numberless eager sprawling bubbling pots and pans. It shone richly. Gazing upon this generous expanse you felt that from its source could emerge nothing that was not savory, nourishing, satisfying.

—Edna Ferber

The wonderful world of home appliances now makes it possible to cook indoors with charcoal and outdoors with gas.

—Bill Vaughan

COOKING GONE TO THE DOGS

Necessity is the mother of invention. In the Middle Ages, European life's stark hardships fostered the growth of communal extended families who shared common living areas, especially the kitchen. The source of food and heat, it became the central room of the home.

With more mouths to feed came the invention which enabled those cooking to prepare large amounts of meat over an open fire—the precursor to the modern barbecue rotisserie—the turnspit. From A.D. 700 to almost 1800, the spit reigned supreme until the invention of the oven.

The original turnspit had one major drawback—turning the spit. Not only did it require physical exertion, the turnspit turned the cook into a music-less, monkey-less organ grinder and away from other pressing responsibilities. Between its inception and Leonardo da Vinci's 16th century invention of a self-turning spit, powered by the rising heat of the fire, many novel ways of turning the spit traipsed through the pages of culinary history including the pooch-powered turnspit.

Leave it to the Brits who in the 1400s devised a pulley system connecting the turnspit with a small wall- or ceiling-mounted cage similar to a very large hamster wheel. Insert one small, hyperactive dog and the spit became automated. A special breed of terrier, appropriately classified as "spit runners", was even developed and trained for the job, giving a whole new meaning to the phrase "dogging it".

Give me the provisions and whole apparatus of a kitchen, and I would starve.

—Michel de Montaigne

The dangerous person in the kitchen is the one who goes rigidly by weights, measurements, thermometers and scales. I would say once more that all these scientific implements are not of much use, the only exception being for making pastry and jams, where exact weights are important.

—X. Marcel Boulestin

A cook is known by his knife.

—Thomas Fuller

In department stores, so much kitchen equipment is bought indiscriminately by people who just come in for men's underwear.

—Julia Child

They were talking in the kitchen, where Catherine had started to prepare a *risotto* with whatever remains she could find. She was mincing some cold meat in her mincing machine, which was called "Beatrice," a strangely gentle and gracious name for the fierce little iron contraption whose strong teeth so ruthlessly pounded up meat and gristle. It always reminded Catherine of an African god with its square head and little short arms, and it was not at all unlike some of the crudely carved images with evil expressions and aggressively pointed breasts which Tom had brought back from Africa.

—Barbara Pym

We [the Chinese] eat food for its texture, the elastic or crisp effect it has on our teeth, as well as for fragrance, flavor and color.

—Lin Yutang

In many ways, chopsticks are the culinary equivalent of the stick shift. They enhance the act of eating and make it more participatory, tactile, not to mention fun. They give a certain ceremony to consumption and force the calorie-conscious diner to focus on the ritual of gustation, and therefore on the amount of food being shoveled into the mouth at any time. This increased awareness, in turn, enhances the attention paid to whatever is being eaten and encourages the diner to focus more on flavor.

—Dena Kleiman

THE ORIGINAL QUICKIE

An anonymous Chinese proverb maintains: "We sit at the table to eat, not to cut up carcasses."

Since antiquity the thought of bringing a cooked animal to the table in anything approximately resembling its original form was considered uncouth. It was also improper to expect a guest to struggle with a meal by having to rend it limb from limb. Such hewing, chopping, and cutting was reserved for the kitchen, out of the sight and mind of those gentle folk at the table. Since the food was already diced into bite-sized pieces, knives at the place settings were unnecessary. The standard eating utensil became the "kwai-tsze" (literally, "quick ones") or, as phonetically butchered by the English, "chopsticks".

Defining a cow:
God's jolly cafeteria
With four legs and a tail.
—Edward Merrill (E.M.) Root

All cooking is a matter of time. In general, the more time the better.
—John Erskine

And there was a cut of some roast...which was borne on Pegasus-wings of garlic beyond mundane speculation.
—C.S. Forester

SOONER OR LATER IT SHALL BE DONE

I shall first begin with roast and boiled of all sorts and must desire the cook to order her fire according to what she is to dress. If any thing very little or thin, then a pretty little brisk fire, that it may be done quick and nice; if a very large joint, then be sure a good fire be laid to cake. Let it be clear at the bottom; and, when your meat is half-done, move the dripping-pan and spit a little from the fire, and stir up a good brisk fire; for, according to the goodness of your fire, your meat will be done sooner or later.

—Hannah Glasse
The Art of Cookery made Plain and Easy (1747; First cookbook written in English by a woman to have achieved any notoriety—was a bestseller in Great Britain for almost 100 years.)

The ingredients of a dish should always harmonize with one another—like two people in a marriage.

—Yuan Mei

Good cooking does not depend on whether the dish is large or small, expensive or economical. If one has the art, then a piece of celery or salted cabbage can be made into a marvelous delicacy; whereas if one has not the art, not all the greatest delicacies and rarities of land, sea or sky are of any avail.

—Yuan Mei

I know that there are people who say that raw materials of the highest order are the key to a good meal. I agree that a perfect peach is a fine thing, and I say also that the decline of the tomato in these United States vitiates the quality of what we eat beyond the rescue of a mere cook's ingenuity. But ... a cook can make a difference.

—Raymond Sokolov

Training is everything. The peach was once a bitter almond; cauliflower is but cabbage with a college education.

—Mark Twain

I saw him even now going the way of all flesh, that is to say towards the kitchen.

—John Webster

When I'm old and gray, I want to have a house by the sea. And paint. With a lot of wonderful chums, good music and booze around. And a damn good kitchen to cook in.

—Ava Gardner

I feel now that gastronomical perfection can be reached in these combinations: one person dining alone, usually upon a couch or hillside; two people of no matter what sex or age, dining in a good restaurant; six people, of no matter what sex or age, dining in a good home.

—M.F.K. Fisher

A man can live for three days without water but not one without poetry.

—Oscar Wilde

Three things are good in little measure and evil in large: yeast, salt, and hesitation.

—Talmud

Birds' nests and water-slugs have no particular flavor of their own, and are therefore not worth eating.

—Yuan Mei

Chamberlain's Law: Everything tastes more or less like chicken.

—Paul Dickson

TIPS ON *PRESERVING BIRDS IN HOT WEATHER...*

To preserve birds not immediately needed for food from going bad in warm or hot weather it is advisable to boil them for at least five minutes with their feathers on.

Do not attempt this until their guts have been drawn, either through the gullet or from the rear.

—Apicius (Marcus Gavius Apicius)
The Roman Cookery Book circa A.D. 14

Poultry is for the cook what canvas is for the painter.

—Brillat-Savarin

I had never touched a raw chicken and it filled me with horror.

—Irene Mayer Selznick

If you are lazy and dump everything together, they won't come out as well as if you add one thing at a time. It's like everything else; no shortcuts without compromising quality.

—Lionel Poilane

As for butter versus margarine, I trust cows more than chemists.

—Joan Gussow

Miss [Julia] Child is never bashful with butter.

—Phil Donahue

The only real stumbling block is fear of failure. In cooking you've got to have a what-the-hell attitude.

—Julia Child

The secret to good cooking resides in the cook's ability to say "the hell with the basic recipe" and improvise freely from it. If you haven't got this kind of moxie, you might as well hang up your apron.

—James Alan McPherson

The qualities of an exceptional cook are akin to those of a successful tight-rope walker: an abiding passion for the task, courage to go out on a limb, and an impeccable sense of balance.

—Bryan Miller

When you become a good cook, you become a good craftsman first. You repeat and repeat and repeat until your hands know how to move without having to think about it.

—Jacques Pépin

Successful cooks do as little as possible to achieve whatever desired results.

—Alan Koehler

Said with regard to his departure for New York City after having been one of 22 French chefs chosen to cook during the centennial celebration of the Statue of Liberty:
I'm taking only my toque blanche and my savoir-faire, (...my white cap and my knowledge).

—Philippe Gaertner

The art of cookery is the art of poisoning mankind, by rendering the appetite still importunate, when the wants of nature are supplied.

—François de Salignac de la Mothe Fénelon

I do not pretend to teach professional cooks, but my design is to instruct the ignorant and unlearned (which will likewise be of great use in all private families), and in so plain and full a manner, that the most illiterate and ignorant person, who can but read, will know how to do every thing in cookery well. [The subtle shades of meaning of the word "illiterate" obviously did not prove an obstacle to being a person "who can but read".]

—Mrs. Hannah Glasse

Plain cooking cannot be entrusted to plain cooks.

—Countess Morphy

Cooks are not to be taught in their own kitchen.

—Thomas Fuller

ALL THAT GLITTERS IS NOT SILVER

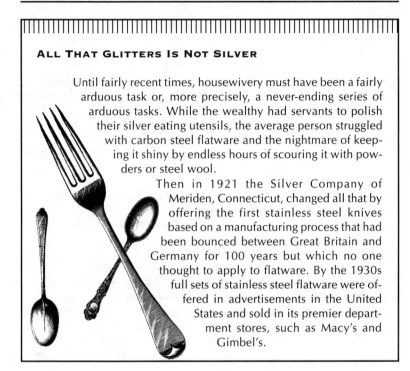

Until fairly recent times, housewivery must have been a fairly arduous task or, more precisely, a never-ending series of arduous tasks. While the wealthy had servants to polish their silver eating utensils, the average person struggled with carbon steel flatware and the nightmare of keeping it shiny by endless hours of scouring it with powders or steel wool.

Then in 1921 the Silver Company of Meriden, Connecticut, changed all that by offering the first stainless steel knives based on a manufacturing process that had been bounced between Great Britain and Germany for 100 years but which no one thought to apply to flatware. By the 1930s full sets of stainless steel flatware were offered in advertisements in the United States and sold in its premier department stores, such as Macy's and Gimbel's.

The more he talked of his honor the faster we counted our spoons.
—Ralph Waldo Emerson

I have the simplest tastes. I am always satisfied with the best.
—Oscar Wilde

Tell me what you eat and I will tell you what you are.

—Brillat-Savarin

If you are what you eat, a visit to North Carolina could make you a very interesting person.

—Advertisement by the North Carolina Travel Department

On meals:
Three a day are recommended. Call me crazy, but if you don't eat you will eventually die.

—John Adler

Statistics show that of those who contract the habit of eating, very few will survive.

—William Wallace Irwin

Health food makes me sick.

—Calvin Trillin

Be careful about reading health books. You may die of a misprint.

—Mark Twain

He had had much experience of physicians, and said "the only way to keep your health is to eat what you don't want, drink what you don't like, and do what you druther not."

—Mark Twain

23

Attention to health is life's greatest hindrance.

—Plato

All I ask of food is that it doesn't harm me.

—Michael Palin

I eat merely to put food out of my mind.

—N.F. Simpson

Some people have a foolish way of not minding, or of pretending not to mind, what they eat. For my part, I mind my belly very studiously and very carefully; for I look upon it that he who does not mind his belly will hardly mind anything else.

—Samuel Johnson

Quit worrying about your health. It'll go away.

—Robert Orben

Health nuts are going to feel stupid someday, lying in hospitals dying of nothing.

—Redd Foxx

I never worry about diets. The only carrots that interest me are the number you get in a diamond.

—Mae West

A RECIPE FOR *COCKSCOMB*: FOR ANY MAN WHO CAN'T KEPP OR KEEP IT UP AT ALL TIMES

Take twelve to seventeen cockscombs, soak them in warm milk until the skins can be easily removed, wash them in cold water until the red pales to a surprising white, sprinkle them with lemon juice (Margaret used pickling liquor), roll the cockscombs in beaten egg, fry them briefly on both sides, and serve them, on rounds of celery root previously sauteed in butter, to any male who, as I did then, has trouble getting and keeping it up and displaying a cocky virility even when he has good reason to hang his head.

—Günter Grass

Thinness is more naked, more indecent, than corpulence.

—Charles Baudelaire

Responding to critics calling her a chain-smoking anorexic supermodel:
Well, I'm not anorexic, but I am a chain-smoker. I try and eat three meals a day. I eat a big breakfast and dinner, and a small lunch. For breakfast I love eggs and bacon; for dinner, Italian food. And there is this brilliant transvestite Thai restaurant in Paris I love going to.

—Kate Moss

Physically [James Beard] was the connoisseur's connoisseur. He was a giant panda, Santa Claus and the Jolly Green Giant rolled into one. On him, a lean and slender physique would have looked like very bad casting.

—Craig Claiborne

A gourmet who thinks of calories is like a tart who looks at her watch.
—James Beard

Oh the glorious town of Konotop glistened with fat! At the market and at the station, behind long rows of tables were mounds of lard of all kinds—smoked and unsmoked with a good rind. There were rings of sausage with a smell so strong it inflamed a man's glands. There was ham rimmed with fat, *kasha* cooked thick with lamb suet and cut into rounds to resemble buns, and country sausage with gristle. The lard-sellers glistened in their greasy clothes, reflecting the rays of the sun.

I'd buy a ring of sausage for five kopecks and break it into pieces, eating it the way people at the market eat. I didn't even glance at the lamb, which cost only a kopeck and a half per pound, nor at the meat. Pork and fish were the best foods at the market, especially the dried searoach at two kopecks a piece, large chunks with fatty red backbone and roe. I liked to eat the pork and the fish with white bread. Or I'd buy a small suckling pig from the lard-seller for forty kopecks—already roasted, with a crisp brown rind stippled with fat. The rind, baked just right, crackled under my teeth. It was easy enough to consume the whole pig in secret from those at home, awaiting me for dinner.

In Konotop, among this Ukrainian fat and garlic, I grew.

—Kazimar Malevich

Back then, nobody knew about cholesterol, and a lot of our food was loaded with it. I still like dishes made with cream and butter. I shouldn't have them, and I'm told it's unhealthy, but *tant pis* (so much the worse).

—Simone Beck

Old World cooking, for the most part, is heavy, and the healthy-food people of our time will simply reject these recipes in the name of flavorless health. Moderation is the answer to a good diet, moderation and flavor and history.

—Jeff Smith (The Frugal Gourmet)

Yoghurt is very good for the stomach, the lumbar regions, appendicitis and apotheosis.

—Eugene Ionesco

God could have created all food as a bland mixture of proper nutrients: something like wheat-germ, yoghurt and honey in a cake form, or some sort of fruit which would have contained everything necessary to good health. However pleasant the mild flavor might be, we cannot imagine eating just one single flavor all the time, the reason being that we have been created with taste buds, a delicate sense of smell, and a sensitive appreciation of and response to texture and colour.

—Edith Schaeffer

I once believed that eating healthy meant eating food that was missing something—TASTE. I once believed eating healthy meant being unsatisfied. I once believed eating healthy meant no security, no comfort, no love.

—Oprah Winfrey

The longer I work in nutrition, the more convinced I become that for the healthy person all foods should be delicious.

—Adele Davis

The *nouvelle cuisine* marked a turning-point. People suddenly understood that they could celebrate without ruining their health.

—Alain Senderens

The first of all considerations is that our meals shall be fun as well as fuel.

—André Simon

Eat, drink, and be merry, for tomorrow we may diet.

—anonymous

THE AMERICAN DIET

As with many things American, the lead for what began the nation's "health-conscious" phenomena came in 1955 when then-President Dwight (Ike) Eisenhower suffered a heart attack while in office. The remedy he prescribed was then followed by many similarly afflicted Americans: "ordered work activity, interspaced with regular amounts of exercise, recreation, and rest." Also on the list was a new attention to diet.

Sermons on diet ought to be preached in the churches at least once a week.

—G.C. Lichtenberg

We are all dietetic sinners; only a small percent of what we eat nourishes us; the balance goes to waste and loss of energy.

—Sir William Osler

Of the ten leading causes of illness and death in the U.S., seven could be greatly reduced if the following lifestyle habits were modified—alcohol abuse, lack of exercise, poor diet, smoking, and unhealthy maladaptive responses to stress and tension.

—Julius B. Richmond

Hunger is not only the best cook, but the best physician.

—Peter Altenberg

If your doctor does not think it good for you to sleep, to drink wine, or to eat of a particular dish, do not worry; I will find you another who will not agree with him.

—Michel de Montaigne

To lengthen life, lessen thy meals.

—Benjamin Franklin

Eighty percent fullness is good for the health.

—Japanese Proverb

One pancake for lunch and half a boiled egg for dinner makes a man at sixty able to do anything a college athlete can do.

—Sir William Osler

Fasting today makes the food good tomorrow.

—German Proverb

If thou rise with an appetite, thou art sure never to sit down without one.

—William Penn

A stomach that is seldom empty despises common food.

—Horace

They are as sick that surfeit with too much, as they that starve with nothing.

—William Shakespeare

One sits the whole day at the desk and appetite is standing next to me. "Away with you," I say. But Comrade Appetite does not budge from the spot.

—Leonid I. Brezhnev

If only it were as easy to banish hunger by rubbing the belly as it is to masturbate.

—Diogenes The Cynic (Diogenes Laertius)

A closed mouth gathers no feet.
—anonymous

No diet will remove all the fat from your body because the brain is entirely fat. Without a brain you might look good, but all you could do is run for public office.

—Covert Bailey

The best way to lose weight is to close your mouth—something very difficult for a politician. Or watch your food—just watch it, don't eat it.

—Edward Koch

If you want to feel important, go on a diet.

—Joey Adams

Oh, my friends, be warned by me,
That breakfast, dinner, lunch and tea
Are all the human frame requires.
—Hilaire Belloc

It is wonderful, if we chose the right diet, what an extraordinarily small quantity would suffice.

—Mohandas Karamchand Gandhi

One meal a day is enough for a lion, and it ought to be enough for a man.

—G. Fordyce

Abstainer: A weak person who yields to the temptation of denying himself a pleasure.

—Ambrose Bierce

Life is too short for cuisine minceur and for diets. Dietetic meals are like an opera without the orchestra.

—Paul Bocuse

On those who prescribe diets:
If they do no other good, they do this at least, that they prepare their patients betimes for death, by gradually undermining and cutting off their enjoyment of life.

—Michel de Montaigne

Old people shouldn't eat health foods. They need all the preservatives they can get.

—Robert Orben

Liquid diets: The powder is mixed with water and tastes exactly like powder mixed with water.

—Art Buchwald

"How long does getting thin take?" Pooh asked anxiously.

—A.A. Milne

RECIPE FOR *PURGING ALE**

Take garden Scurvey-Grass, Burdock-Roots bruised, and blew Currants, of each half a Pound.

Of Rhubarb slic'd, and Horse-Radish roots, scrap'd, each an Ounce and a half. The Roots of Monks-Rhubarb, sharp-pointed Dock, of each three Ounces and a half. Of Mechoacan, and Senna, three Ounces and a half.

Coriander-Seeds, each an Ounce and a half; with three Oranges sliced.

Put all these Ingredients into a Canvas-Bag, with a Stone in it, and hang it in three Gallons of new Ale, and let them work fierce together.

In three Days time it will be drinkable: take a Pint for a Morning's draught.

[*The purpose of which was to "fast cleanse the bowels of such as be costive" to be enjoyed only while actually sitting on the privy or closet-house "if privy or closet-house there be."]

—John Nott, *The Cook's and Confectioner's Dictionary; or, the Accomplished Housewife's Companion* (1723)

Eat as much as you like—just don't swallow.

—Steve Burns

I know a man who gave up smoking, drinking, sex, and rich food. He was healthy right up to the time he killed himself.

—Johnny Carson

Never eat more than you can lift.
—Miss Piggy

The appetites of the belly and the palate, far from diminishing as men grow older, go on increasing.

—Cicero

The only way to get thin is to reestablish a purpose in life.

—Cyril Connolly

If you want to look young and thin, hang around old fat people.

—Jim Eason

I've been on a diet for two weeks and all I've lost is two weeks.

—Totie Fields

Dieting is murder on the road. Show me a man who travels and I'll show you one who eats.

—Bruce Froemming

When a man diets, he eats oatmeal in addition to everything else he usually eats.

—E.W. Howe

Mammy to Scarlett O'Hara:
Young misses whut eats heavy mos' gener'ly doan never ketch husbands.
—Margaret Mitchell

We connive to keep the calories down and feel triumphant when we get compliments on a low-calorie meal from the man we are trying to please.

—Lady Bird Johnson

From time to time I did get one or two letters pleading, "Don't you use a little too much butter and cream?" My serious answer to that was, "Madam, you could get run over by a bus and just think what you would have missed!" And then came the jolt. My wife, Treena, suddenly had serious heart problems. She hadn't been run over by a bus but she had been buttered and creamed by the way we had been eating!

—Graham Kerr

I feel about diets the way I feel about airplanes. They're wonderful things for other people to go on.

—Jean Kerr

If you have formed the habit of checking on every new diet that comes along, you will find that, mercifully, they all blur together, leaving you with only one definite piece of information: french-fried potatoes are out.

—Jean Kerr

The best way to lose weight is to get the flu and take a trip to Egypt.

—Roz Lawrence

If you wish to grow thinner, diminish your dinner,
And take to light claret instead of pale ale;
Look down with an utter contempt upon butter
And never touch bread till it's toasted—or stale.

—H.S. Leigh

A vegetarian is a person who won't eat anything that can have children.

—David Brenner

In America, the cow is on trial. The charges include dietary wrongdoing, pollution and misuse of natural resources.

—Molly O'Neill

When mighty roast beef was the Englishman's food,
It ennobled our hearts and enriched our blood,
Our soldiers were brave and courtiers good,
Oh! The roast beef of old England!

—Richard Leveridge

***THE HEALING PROP-
ERTIES OF TEA AND
COFFEE***

The medical properties of
these two beverages are
considerable. Tea is used
advantageously in inflam-
matory diseases and as a
cure for the headache.
Coffee is supposed to act
as a preventative of gravel
and gout, and to its influence is ascribed the rarity
of those diseases in France
and Turkey. Both tea and

coffee counteract the effects of opium and intoxicating liquors;
though, when taken in excess, and without nourishing food, they
themselves produce, temporarily at least, some of the more disagreeable consequences incident to the use of ardent spirits. In
general, however, none but persons possessing great mobility of
the nervous system, or enfeebled or effeminate constitutions, are
injuriously affected by the moderate use of tea and coffee in connection with food.

—Hugo Ziemann, Steward of the White House,
and Mrs. F.L. Gillette, *The Original White House Cookbook:
Contains Cooking, Toilet and Household Recipes, Menus,
Dinner-giving, Table Etiquette, Care of the Sick, Health Suggestions, Facts Worth Knowing, etc.* (1887)

Greater eaters of meat are in general more cruel and ferocious than other men.

—Jean-Jacques Rousseau

Most vegetarians I ever see looked enough like their food to be classed as cannibals.

—Finley Peter Dunne

Doth not the appetite alter? A man loves the meat in his youth that he cannot endure in his age.

—William Shakespeare

Much meat, much malady.

—Thomas Fuller

I am a great eater of beef, and I believe that it does harm to my wit.

—William Shakespeare

The Norman takes his vegetables in the form of animals. "Herbivores eat grass," one hotel landlord told me. "Man, a carnivore, eats herbivores."

—A.J. Liebling

Give them great meals of beef and iron and steel, they will act like wolves and fight like devils.

—William Shakespeare

It is nearly fifty years since I was assured by a conclave of doctors that if I did not eat meat I should die of starvation.

—George Bernard Shaw

If any man has drunk a little too deeply from the cup of physical pleasure; if he has spent too much time at his desk that should have been spent asleep; if his fine spirits have become temporarily dulled; if he finds the air too damp, the minutes too slow, and the atmosphere too heavy to withstand; if he is obsessed by a fixed idea which bars him from any freedom of thought: if he is any of these poor creatures, we say, let him be given a good pint of amber-flavoured chocolate...and marvels will be performed.

—Brillat-Savarin

AN EARLY WARNING FOR THE OVERWORKED...

Let a man go home, tired or exhausted, eat a full supper of starchy and vegetable food, occupy his mind intently for a while, go to bed in a warm, close room, and if he doesn't have a cold in the morning it will be a wonder. A drink or two of whisky or a glass or two of beer before supper will facilitate matters very much.

—Hugo Ziemann, Steward of the White House, and Mrs. F.L. Gillette, *The Original White House Cookbook: Contains Cooking, Toilet and Household Recipes, Menus, Dinner-giving, Table Etiquette, Care of the Sick, Health Suggestions, Facts Worth Knowing, etc.* (1887)

Pounding fragrant things—particularly garlic, basil, parsley—is a tremendous antidote to depression. But it applies also to juniper berries, coriander seeds and the grilled fruits of the chili pepper. Pounding these things produces an alteration in one's being—from sighing with fatigue to inhaling with pleasure. The cheering effects of herbs and alliums cannot be too often reiterated. Virgil's appetite was probably improved equally by pounding garlic as by eating it.

—Patience Gray

Wine is the most healthful and most hygienic of beverages.

—Louis Pasteur

JUST DON'T SWALLOW...

People swallow more colds down their throats than they inhale or receive from contact with the air, no matter how cold or chilly it may be. Plain, light suppers are good to go to bed on, and are far more conducive to refreshing sleep than a glass of beer or a dose of chloral. In the estimation of a great many this statement is rank heresy, but in the light of science, common sense and experience it is gospel truth.

—Hugo Ziemann, Steward of the White House, and Mrs. F.L. Gillette, *The Original White House Cookbook: Contains Cooking, Toilet and Household Recipes, Menus, Dinner-giving, Table Etiquette, Care of the Sick, Health Suggestions, Facts Worth Knowing, etc.* (1887)

The secret of staying young is to live honestly, eat slowly, and lie about your age.

—Lucille Ball

Just as eating contrary to the inclination is injurious to the health, so study without desire spoils the memory, and it retains nothing that it takes in.

—Leonardo da Vinci

What one relishes, nourishes.

—Benjamin Franklin

An apple a day keeps the doctor away.

—anonymous

Human beings do not eat nutrients, they eat food.

—Mary Catherine Bateson

He who takes medicine and neglects to diet wastes the skill of his doctors.

—Chinese Proverb

It is the part of a wise man to feed himself with moderate pleasant food and drink, and to take pleasure with perfumes, with the beauty of growing plants, dress, music, sports, and theatres and other places of this kind which a man may use without any hurt to his fellows.

—Spinoza

One of "those" bumper stickers:
Cooks do it with taste.

—anonymous

People care more about being thought to have good taste than about being thought either good, clever, or amiable.

—Samuel Butler

Men lose their tempers in defending their taste.

—Ralph Waldo Emerson

**Good taste is the worst vice ever invented.
—Edith Sitwell**

The kind of people who always go on about whether a thing is in good taste invariably have very bad taste.

—Joe Orton

Etiquette means behaving yourself a little better than is absolutely essential.

—Will Cuppy

When our integrity declines, our taste does also.

—La Rochefoucauld

The less I behave like Whistler's mother the night before, the more I look like her the morning after.

—Tallulah Bankhead

In every power, of which taste is the foundation, excellence is pretty fairly divided between the sexes.

—Jane Austen

Breaking a glass in the northwest [Australia] is rather like belching in Arabia, for it appears to be done as a mark of appreciation or elation.

—Jonathan Aitken

On eating dinner with King Ibn Saud of Saudi Arabia, who, as a practicing Moslem, abstained from drinking and smoking:
My rule of life prescribed as an absolutely sacred rite smoking cigars and also the drinking of alcohol before, after and if need be during all meals and in the intervals in between them.

—Winston S. Churchill

To be sure, it is a shocking thing, blowing smoke out of our mouths into other people's mouths, eyes, and noses, and having the same done to us.

—Samuel Johnson

At a dinner party one should eat wisely but not too well, and talk well but not too wisely.

—W. Somerset Maugham

I prefer the Chinese method of eating....You can do anything at the table except arm wrestle.

—Jeff Smith (The Frugal Gourmet)

On entertaining: Serve the dinner backward, do anything—but for goodenss sake, do something weird.

—Elsa Maxwell

NO LIPSMACKING ALLOWED

Be careful to keep the mouth shut closely while masticating the food. It is the opening of the lips which causes the smacking which seems very disgusting.

—Hugo Ziemann, Steward of the White House, and Mrs. F.L. Gillette, *The Original White House Cookbook: Cooking, Toilet and Household Recipes, Dinner-giving, Table Etiquette, Care of the Health Suggestions, Facts Worth Knowing* (1887)

The Saxons needed no excuse for a feast. They ate as often as they could, and drank mighty drafts of foaming mead and ale. Over the carcass of the boar they passed around horn drinking tumblers that had pointed bases and so could not be put down until the last drop was drained. This was story time, and from such feasts our English literature was born. While the flames of the fire cast dancing shadows on the walls, men would repeat the old tale of Beowulf and his fight with the monster Grendel, who lived with his mother at the bottom of the lake.

—Adrian Bailey

The more the merrier; the fewer, the better fare.

—John Palsgrave

Some people are alarmed if the company are thirteen in number. The number is only to be dreaded when the dinner is provided for but twelve.

—Lancelot Sturgeon

I write these precepts for immortal Greece, that round a table delicately spread, three or four may sit in choice repast, or five at most. Who otherwise shall dine, are like a troop marauding for their prey.

—Archestratus

Crowd not your table: let your numbers be
Not more than seven, and never less than three.
—King William IV of England

At a round table there's no dispute of place.

—John Ray

I don't care where I sit as long as I get fed.

—Calvin Trillin

It is equally wrong to speed a guest who does not want to go, and to keep one back who is eager. You ought to make welcome the present guest, and send forth the one who wishes to go.

—Homer

And most dear actors, eat no onion nor garlic for we are to utter sweet breath.

—William Shakespeare

Maybe ain't ain't so correct, but I notice that lots of folks who ain't using ain't ain't eatin'.

—Will Rogers

Mr. Desmond MacCarthy has said that the hallmark of Bohemianism is a tendency to use things for purposes to which they are not adapted. You are a Bohemian, says Mr. MacCarthy, if you would gladly use a razor for buttering your toast at breakfast, and you aren't if you wouldn't.

—Max Beerbohm

On being a professional chef:
It was never considered a glamourous profession. Not until "executive-chef" was reclassified as a white-collar job and chefs began to be celebratized, did it become more desirable.

—Patrick Clark

Everything depended upon things being served up the precise moment they were ready. The beef, the bay leaf, and the wine—all must be done to a turn. To keep it waiting was out of the question. Yet of course tonight, of all nights, out they went, and they came in late, and things had to be kept hot; the Boeuf en Daube would be entirely spoilt.

—Virginia Woolf

While cooking, do not allow ashes from your pipe, perspiration from your face, soot from the fuel, or beetles from the ceiling to drop into the saucepan: the guests would be likely to pass the dish by.

—Yuan Mei

He is a sorry cook that may not lick his own finger.

—John Ray

To be without a sense of taste is to be deficient in an exquisite faculty, that of appreciating the qualities of food, just as a person may lack the faculty of appreciating the quality of a book or a work of art. It is to want a vital sense, one of the elements of human superiority.

—Guy de Maupassant

Our tastes often improve at the expense of our happiness.

—Jules Renard

It took over two hundred years to develop a good base of cooking and we shouldn't forget it just for the sake of change.

—André Soltner

On nouvelle cuisine:
A plate doesn't have to be arranged like an abstract painting.

—Larry Forgione

ALAS, POOR YORKSHIRE, I KNEW HIM WELL...

Do not attempt to eulogize your dishes, or apologize that you cannot recommend them— this is extreme bad taste; as also is the vaunting of the excellence of your wines, etc., etc.

—Hugo Ziemann, Steward of the White House, and Mrs. F.L. Gillette, *The Original White House Cookbook: Contains Cooking, Toilet and Household Recipes, Menus, Dinner-giving, Table Etiquette, Care of the Sick, Health Suggestions, Facts Worth Knowing, etc.* (1887)

There is nothing more horrible than imagination without taste.

—Goethe

First flowers on the table; then food.

—Danish Proverb

If I have not wrote [my cook book] in the high, polite Stile, I hope I shall be forgiven; for my Intention is to instruct the lower sort, and therefore must treat them in their own Way....So in many other things in Cookery, the great Cooks have such a high way of expressing themselves, that the poor Girls are at a Loss to know what they mean. In all Receipt [recipe] Books yet printed, there are such an odd Jumble of things as would quite spoil *a good dish.*

—Mrs. Hannah Glasse

I seem to you cruel and gluttonous, when I beat my cook for sending up a bad dinner. If that appears to you too trifling a cause, say for what cause you would have a cook flogged?

—Martial

Eating is an activity to which just about everyone brings a roughly equal body of experience and opinion, along with the inherited set of prejudices and preferences that even the most cosmopolitan diner never quite relinquishes. Like Charles Shulz's Linus, we all carry a security blanket stained by the accidents of our earliest eating experiences.

—Jay Jacobs

On being a Mafia cook:
Now, mobsters love to eat. They eat while planning crimes and they eat after committing crimes, and when there are no crimes, they eat while waiting for them to happen. And mobsters are very picky. They know what they like, and when they like it they eat all of it. And then more. Look at the stomachs on these guys the next time television shows one of them being escorted into court in handcuffs. These are some very serious eaters....Remember the crowd I was feeding—any meal may be their last, so it better be a good one. Crime may not pay, but it sure gives you a hell of an appetite.

—Joseph (Joe Dogs) Iannuzzi

A GREAT ANNOYANCE

Do not insist upon your guests partaking of particular dishes. Do not ask persons more than once, and never force a supply upon their plates. It is ill-bred, though common, to press any one to eat; and, moreover, it is a great annoyance to many.

—Hugo Ziemann, Steward of the White House, and Mrs. F.L. Gillette, *The Original White House Cookbook: Contains Cooking, Toilet and Household Recipes, Menus, Dinner-giving, Table Etiquette, Care of the Sick, Health Suggestions, Facts Worth Knowing, etc.* (1887)

BREAKFAST

One morning in November I awoke at 6:30 a.m. and looked out on a gray landscape that would have dispirited Gustave Doré: palpably damp, lunar in its deleafed desolation, it made my bone marrow feel as though I somehow had extracted it and left it in a dish on the back step all night. It was one of those mornings when a man could face the day only after warming himself with a mug of thick coffee beaded with steam, a good thick crust of bread, and bowl of bean soup.

—Richard Gehman

> **BREAKFAST IS A FORECAST OF THE WHOLE DAY:**
> **SPOIL THAT AND ALL IS SPOILED.**
> **—LEIGH HUNT**

Early rising is also essential to the good government of a family. A late breakfast deranges the whole business of the day and throws a portion of it into the next, which opens the door for confusion to enter.

—Martha Jefferson Randolph

Never work before breakfast; if you have to work before breakfast, eat your breakfast first.

—Josh Billings

All happiness depends on a leisurely breakfast.

—John Gunther

I am one who eats breakfast gazing at morning glories.

—Basho

Nothing helps scenery like ham and eggs.

—Mark Twain

My wife and I tried two or three times in the last 40 years to have breakfast together, but it was so disagreeable we had to stop.

—Winston S. Churchill

A simple enough pleasure, surely, to have breakfast alone with one's husband, but how seldom married people in the midst of life achieve it.

—Anne Morrow Lindbergh

The breakfast table is not a bulletin board for the curing of horrible dreams and depressing symptoms, but the place where a bright keynote for the day is struck.

—B.G. Jeffries

Only dull people are brilliant at breakfast.

—Oscar Wilde

Breakfast is a notoriously difficult meal to serve with a flourish.

—Clement Freud

Every morning one must start from scratch with nothing on the stoves. That is cuisine.

—Fernand Point

I grew up eating well. Cheese grits, homemade biscuits smothered in butter, home-cured ham, red-eyed gravy—and that was just breakfast.

—Oprah Winfrey

Life, within doors, has few pleasanter prospects than a neatly arranged and well-provisioned breakfast table.

—Nathaniel Hawthorne

A RECIPE FOR *HASH:*
THE INITIAL INSTRUCTIONS FOR
THE COOKS WHO SERVED KING
RICHARD II

Take hares and hew them to gobbletts...
Take conies and smite them to pieces...
Take chickens and ram them together.
  —anonymous, *The Forme of Cury*
  (14th century British cookbook)

Oysters are the usual opening to a winter breakfast....Indeed, they are almost indispensable.

—Grimod de la Reynière

You have to eat oatmeal or you'll dry up. Anybody knows that.

—Kay Thompson

The breakfast of champions is not cereal, it's the opposition.

—Nick Seitz

There are certain tastes which those who have never experienced them as children can neither understand nor cure: who but an Englishman, for example, can know the delights of stone-cold leathery toast for breakfast, or the wonders of "Dead Man's Leg"?

—W.H. Auden

To eat well in England, you should have a breakfast three times a day.

—W. Somerset Maugham

What? Sunday morning in an English family and no sausage? God bless my soul, what's the world coming to, eh?

—Dorothy Sayers

A highbrow is the kind of person who looks at a sausage and thinks of Picasso.

—A.P. Herbert

Laws are like sausages. It's better not to see them being made.

—Otto von Bismarck

Last words:
Doctor, do you think it could have been the sausage?

—Paul Claudel

On the introduction of leaner sausages:
You're going out on a dangerous limb, making healthy sausages.

—Stanley Hunt

> Bring porridge, bring sausage, bring fish for a start,
> Bring kidneys and mushrooms and partridges' legs,
> But let the foundation be bacon and eggs.

—A.P. Herbert

The flavor of frying bacon beats orange blossoms.

—E.W. Howe

On the egg:
In shape, it is perfectly elliptical. In texture, it is smooth and lustrous. In color, it ranges from pale alabaster to warm terra cotta. And in taste, it outstrips all the lush pomegranates that Swinburne was so fond of sinking his lyrical teeth into.

—Sydney J. Harris

I'm frightened of eggs, worse than frightened, they revolt me. That white round thing without any holes...have you ever seen anything more revolting than an egg yolk breaking and spilling its yellow liquid? Blood is jolly, red. But egg yolk is yellow, revolting. I've never tasted it.

—Alfred Hitchcock

> **Most men are like eggs, too full of themselves to hold anything else.**
> **—Josh Billings**

The breakfast egg was a Victorian institution (only a century old); whatever else there was for breakfast—kidneys, chops, bacon, or kedgeree, with tea or coffee, marmalade or honey—there was always a meek little cluster of boiled eggs, set modestly apart upon a chased silver stand, with their spoons beside them (like St. Ursula's virgins on shipboard).

—Dorothy Hartley

Omelettes are not made without breaking eggs.

—Robespierre

Be content to remember that those who can make omelettes properly can do nothing else.

—Hilaire Belloc

As everybody knows, there is only one infallible recipe for the perfect omelette: your own.

—Elizabeth David

He placed the letter on the pile beside his plate; and, having decapitated an egg, peered sharply into its interior as if hoping to surprise guilty secrets.

—P.G. Wodehouse

The hen is only an egg's way of producing another egg.

—Samuel Butler

I had an excellent repast—the best possible repast—which consisted simply of boiled eggs and bread and butter. It was the quality of these simple ingredients that made the occasion memorable. The eggs were so good that I am ashamed to say how many of them I consumed....It might seem that an egg which has succeeded in being fresh has done all that can be reasonably expected of it.

—Henry James

If I were given my choice between an egg and ambrosia for breakfast, I should choose an egg.

—Robert Lynd

•

On diner menus:
It is beyond the imagination of the menu-maker that there are people in the world who breakfast on a single egg.

—Melvin Maddocks

Put all thine eggs in one basket and—watch that basket.

—Mark Twain

My cow milks me.

—Ralph Waldo Emerson

All is not butter that comes from the cow.

—Thomas Fuller

HOW MUCH BUTTER?

I have heard of a Cook that used six pounds of butter to fry twelve Eggs; when every Body knows (that understands Cooking) that Half a Pound of Butter is full enough—or more than need be used. But then it would not be French!

—Mrs. Hannah Glasse , *The Art of Cookery made Plain and Easy* (1747; First cookbook written in English by a woman to have achieved any notoriety—was a bestseller in Great Britain for almost 100 years.)

Bread, milk and butter are of venerable antiquity. The taste of the morning of the world.

—Leigh Hunt

I said my prayers and ate some cranberry tart for breakfast.

—William Byrd

PRESIDENTIAL PANCAKES.

The American White House has long been a bastion for the lowly breakfast pancake. Thomas Jefferson, that famous egalitarian and common man, was so insistent that he be served his favorite "batter cakes, fried apples, and hot breads served with bacon and eggs" done to perfection for breakfast that he had his governess brought up from his Monticello home to the White House. Andrew Jackson, in keeping with his rugged, individualist self, preferred buckwheat-cornmeal flapjacks with hot molasses or buttered maple syrup. "Silent" Calvin Coolidge, as well as being tight with words, may have been the original frugal gourmet, scheduling meetings at breakfast where he regaled White House guests and dignitaries with economical buckwheat cakes and Vermont maple syrup. FDR favored plain old pancakes with hot buttered maple syrup and Ike, his tastes no doubt permanently scarred by army food, went for cornmeal cakes drowned in light molasses.

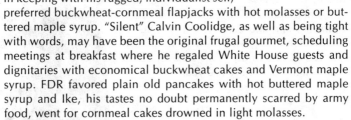

It is as healthy to enjoy sentiment as to enjoy jam.

—G.K. Chesterton

Marmalade in the morning has the same effect on taste buds that a cold shower has on the body.

—Jeanne Larmoth

You don't get tired of muffins, but you don't find inspiration in them.

—George Bernard Shaw

The cheery noise of bubbling pancake batter was as plainly heard as the singing teakettle every morning of the year in our house. I often lifted the cover of the batter crock to look at the bubbles, which reminded me of the eyes of animals.

—U.P. Hedrick

A day without orange juice is like a day without sunshine.

—Advertisement for the Florida Citrus Commission

Push right to the extreme and it becomes wrong: press all the juice from an orange and it becomes bitter.

—Baltasar Gracían

The morning cup of coffee has an exhilaration about it which the cheering influence of the afternoon or evening cup of tea cannot be expected to reproduce.

—Oliver Wendell Holmes, Sr.

Cocoa? Cocoa! Damn miserable puny stuff, fit for kittens and unwashed boys. Did *Shakespeare* drink cocoa?

—Shirley Jackson

I was so darned sorry for poor old Corky that I hadn't the heart to touch my breakfast. I told Jeeves to drink it himself.

—P.G. Wodehouse

LUNCH

We were taken to a fast-food café where our order was fed into a computer. Our hamburger, made from the flesh of chemically impregnated cattle, had been broiled over counterfeit charcoal, placed between slices of artificially flavored cardboard and served to us by recycled juvenile delinquents.

—Jean Michel Chapereau

A hamburger is warm and fragrant and juicy. A hamburger is soft and non-threatening. It personifies the Great Mother herself who has nourished us from the beginning. A hamburger is an icon of layered circles, the circle being at once the most spiritual and the most sensual of shapes. A hamburger is companionable and faintly erotic. The nipple of the Goddess, the bountiful belly-ball of Eve. You are what you think you eat.

—Tom Robbins

It is the Americans who have managed to crown minced beef as hamburger, and to send it round the world so that even the fussy French have taken to *le boeuf haché, le hambourgaire.*

—Julia Child

Anybody who doesn't think that the best hamburger place in the world is in his home town is a sissy.

—Calvin Trillin

Rock and roll is the hamburger that ate the world.

—Peter York

There's a lot more future in hamburgers than in baseball. Baseball isn't baseball anymore.

—Ray Kroc

Sacred cows make the tastiest hamburger.
—Abbie Hoffman

Las Vegas is Everyman's cut-rate Babylon. Not far away there is, or was, a roadside lunch counter and over it a sign proclaiming in three words that a Roman emperor's orgy is now a democratic institution...."Topless Pizza Lunch."

—Alistair Cooke

One of the main glories of New York is its ethnic food, and only McDonald's and Burger King equalize us all.

—John Corry

New York is the greatest city in the world for lunch...That's the gregarious time. And when that first martini hits the liver like a silver bullet, there is a sigh of contentment that can be heard in Dubuque.

—William Emerson, Jr.

When ordering lunch, the big executives are just as indecisive as the rest of us.

—William C. Feather

Describing his company:
A Federal Express of fast food.

—John Jay Hooker, *Hooker's Hamburgers*

As life's pleasures go, food is second only to sex. Except for salami and eggs. Now that's better than sex, but only if the salami is thickly sliced.

—Alan King

The perfect lover is one who turns into a pizza at 4:00 a.m.

—Charles Pierce

Believe it or not, Americans eat 75 *acres* of pizza a day.

—Boyd Matson

A shady spot takes his fancy; soft grass welcomes him, and the murmur of the nearby spring invites him to deposit in its cool waters the flask of wine destined to refresh him. Then, with calm contentment, he takes out of his knapsack the cold chicken and golden-crusted rolls packed for him by loving hands, and places them beside the wedge of Gruyère or Roquefort which is to serve as his dessert.

—Brillat-Savarin

Let us consider for a moment lunch in the country. I do not mean lunch in the open air, for it is obvious that there is no meal so heavenly as lunch thus eaten, and I have no time to dwell upon the obvious.

—A.A. Milne

LUNCH ON THE RUN...*TEA WITH EGGS*

To near a pint of the infusion, take two yolks of new-laid eggs, and beat them very well with as much fine sugar as is sufficient for this quantity of liquor.

When they are well incorporated, pour your Tea upon the Eggs and Sugar, and stir them well together. So drink it hot!

This drink is cordial to health when you come home from attending business abroad, and are very hungry, and yet have not conveniency to eat at once a competent meal. You will find this presently dissolveth and satisfieth all rawness and indigence of the stomach, and flyeth suddenly over the whole body and into the veins, and strengtheneth exceedingly, and preserves one a good while from the necessity of eating.

—Sir Kenelm Digby, *The Sir Kenelm Digby Kt, Opened: Several Ways of Making Cherry Wine, etc. Together with Directions for Cookery—also for Preserving, Conserving, Candying, etc.* (1669). From the essay "Tea with Eggs"

Closet of the Eminently Learned Whereby is Discovered Metheglin, Sider, Excellent

Bologna is celebrated for producing popes, painters, and sausages.

—Lord Byron

The frankfurter had a rubber skin, of course, and my temporary teeth weren't much of a fit. I had to do kind of a sawing movement before I could get my teeth through the skin. And then suddenly—pop! The thing burst in my mouth like a rotten pear. A sort of horrible soft stuff was oozing over my tongue. But the taste! For a moment I just couldn't believe it! Then I rolled my tongue around it again and had another try. It was fish! A sausage, a thing calling itself a frankfurter filled with fish! I got up and walked straight out without touching my coffee. God knows what that might have tasted of.

—George Orwell

They [the men who robbed his famous New York delicatessen] didn't even have enough brains to take a couple of good pastrami sandwiches.

—Leo Steiner

Book title:
A Hero Ain't Nothin' But a Sandwich

—Alice Childress

On eating snake meat:
Boy, the things I do for England.

—Prince Charles

ENTERTAINING: HIGH TEA & OTHER MIDDAY DIVERSIONS

Give the guest food to eat even though you yourself are starving. What is pleasanter than the tie of host and guest?

—Aeschylus

The hostess must be like the duck—calm and unruffled on the surface, and paddling like hell underneath.

—anonymous

Be attentive and receptive to guests. A true man expresses his dignity not only in combat, but how he treats his fellow human. You can be dying from fatigue, but never let it show to a guest. Always be modest about yourself and curious about the guest.

—Kazakh Proverb

On hosting parties:
They make me feel like a stranger in my own house. I look around, make sure everyone is speaking, everyone is fed, everything seems comfortable, see there is no melodrama, then I try to relax. Then I remember this is not the occasion to relax.

—Giorgio Armani

For a single woman, preparing for company means wiping the lipstick off the milk carton.

—Elayne Boosler

Mankind is divisible into two great classes: hosts and guests.

—Max Beerbohm

To mankind in general Macbeth and Lady Macbeth stand out as the supreme type of all that a host and hostess should not be.

—Max Beerbohm

On entertaining and responsibilities of diplomacy quoted at a dinner given by the Association of Southeast Asian Nations:
Today we had a lunch for Jaime de Piniés, the president of the General Assembly, then we had cocktails with the foreign minister of Austria. We passed through a Chinese dinner, and now we are here. It's our life.

—Otilia Barbosa de Medina

DINNER WITH THE JACKSONS

President Andrew Jackson had a reputation for quick-witted snubs. One such story took place as he was preparing to fight the Battle of New Orleans during the War of 1812.

Prior to the battle itself and to Christmas, a report Jackson received from British Admiral Cochrane boasted, "I shall eat my Christmas dinner in New Orleans." To which Jackson replied, "Perhaps so; but I shall have the honor of presiding at that dinner."

If you accept a dinner invitation—you have a moral obligation to be amusing.
—Wallis Simpson (Duchess of Windsor)

The world, like an accomplished hostess, pays most attention to those whom it will soonest forget.

—John Churton Collins

On his 80th birthday:
My dinners have never interfered with my business. They have been my recreation....A public banquet, if eaten with thought and care, is no more of a strain than a dinner at home.

—Chauncey Depew

Hostesses who entertain much must make up their parties as [government] ministers make up their cabinets, on grounds other than personal liking.
—George Eliot (Marian Evans Cross)

Hospitality consists in a little fire, a little food, and an immense quiet.
—Ralph Waldo Emerson

Fish and visitors stink in three days.

—Benjamin Franklin

Some people stay longer in an hour than others do in a month.
—William Dean Howells

The chickens we raised were also propitious. They were as free-range as any *poularde de Bresse* and twice as big as a Perdue. These were chickens to put meat on your bones, and if they were old enough to be tough, we cooked them long enough to weaken their resistance. A Christmas chicken had to be big enough to serve six people one piece each, with wings, back, neck, and pope's nose available upon request. Nothing went to waste, including the wishbone. As the youngest, I claimed the wishbone as my birthright and let it dry on my butter plate during dinner so that it would be brittle enough for wishing on after dessert. I chose Grandfather for my wishmate because I knew that at the last moment he would slip his thumb down his side of the bone to break it first so that my wish would come true. My wishbone wish was the same as my bedtime prayer: "Make me a good girl and let me be happy." I was too young to know what an oxymoron was.

—Betty Fussell

RECIPE FOR TURKEY SOUP TO GO

Obtain a gross of small white boxes such as are used for a bride's cake. Cut the turkey into small squares, roast, stuff, kill, boil, bake, and allow to skewer. Now we are ready to begin. Fill each box with a quantity of soup stock and pile in a handy place. As the liquid elapses, the prepared turkey is added until the guests arrive. The boxes delicately tied with white ribbons are then placed in the handbags of the ladies, or in the men's sidepockets.

—F. Scott Fitzgerald

There never was such a goose. Bob said he didn't believe there ever was such a goose cooked. Its tenderness and flavor, size and cheapness were the themes of universal admiration. Eked out by apple-sauce and mashed potatoes, it was a sufficient dinner for the whole family; indeed, as Mrs. Cratchit said with great delight (surveying one small atom of a bone upon the dish) they hadn't ate it all at last! Yet every one had had enough, and the youngest Crachits in particular were steeped in sage and onion to the eyebrows.

—Charles Dickens

For my grandfather it was not Christmas unless he had his *pichon*. I have never seen anyone eat pigeon or squab the way my grandfather did. I would watch with fascination as he consumed the birds in a methodical way, with a sense of perfection a surgeon would envy. Each bone was picked completely clean, and they had an almost polished look when he was finished. He would arrange them on his plate, again with a perfection that seemed almost architectural. His pigeon made him so happy. A great grin would spread over his face when he was finished, and he would nod to all of us at the table with a look we'd not see again until next Christmas, and his next pigeon.

—Felipe Rojas-Lombardi

Now to the banquet we press;
   Now for the eggs, the ham,
Now for the mustard and cress,
   Now for the strawberry jam!
Now for the tea of our host,
   Now for the rollicking bun,
Now for the muffin and toast,
   Now for the gay Sally Lunn!

—W.S. Gilbert

Modesty is unbecoming a cook and only stimulates the critical faculties of guests.

—Anna Haycroft

In my experience, clever food is not appreciated at Christmas. It makes the little ones cry and the old ones nervous.

—Oliver Wendell Holmes, Sr.

> *The true essentials of a feast are only fun and feed.*
> *—Oliver Wendell Holmes, Sr.*

A host is like a general: it takes a mishap to reveal his genius.

—Horace

On being a Mafia cook:
I like to cook. I've always liked to cook. That is, as long as I didn't have to cook, I liked it. It was when I was made to cook I hated it, because if I didn't do it they'd either fire me or, later, fire at me.

—Joseph (Joe Dogs) Iannuzzi

The pleasure in giving a dinner is mostly the pleasure of giving yourself. The effort you take is your way of showing your company that you care about them enough to give them a good time.

—Marguerite Kelly and Elia Parsons

[I]f it doesn't look, smell, taste, and feel fantastic, it won't bring them back for a second visit.

—Graham Kerr

It is entirely too folksy to serve your own cookies in your own house at any time.

—Alan Koehler

One more drink and I'll be under the host.
—Dorothy Parker

At table people enjoy one another; above all when one has managed to enchant them.

—Fernand Point

One of a hostess's duties is to act as a procuress.

—Marcel Proust

Who depends upon another man's table often dines late.

—John Ray

For a rich man the finest role in the world is that of host.

—Grimod de la Reynière

A freeloader is a confirmed guest.

—Damon Runyon

He hath eaten me out of house and home.

—William Shakespeare

Unbidden guests
Are often welcomest when they are gone.
—William Shakespeare

Small cheer and great welcome makes a merry feast.

—William Shakespeare

The king and high priest of all the festivals was the autumn Thanksgiving. When the apples were all gathered and the cider was all made, and the yellow pumpkins were rolled in from many a hill in billows of gold, and the corn was husked, and the labors of the season were done, and the warm, late days of Indian Summer came in, dreamy, and calm, and still, with just enough frost to crisp the ground of a morning, but with warm traces of benignant, sunny hours at noon, there came over the community a sort of genial repose of spirit—a sense of something accomplished.

—Harriet Beecher Stowe

Recalling the first Thanksgiving celebration in Plymouth, MA:
Our harvest being gotten in, our Governor sent four men on fowling, so that we might after a special manner rejoice together after we had gathered the fruit of our labor. They four in one day killed as much fowl as, with a little help beside, served the company almost a week. At which time, amongst other recreations, we exercised our arms, many of the Indians coming among us, and among the rest their greatest King Massasoit, with some ninety men, whom for three days we entertained and feasted, and they went out and killed five deer, which they brought to the plantation and bestowed on our Governor, and upon the captain, and others.

—Edward Winslow

Conversation is but carving!
Give no more to every guest
Than he's able to digest.
Give him always of the prime,
And but little at a time.
Carve to all but just enough,
Let them neither starve nor stuff,
And that you may have your due,
Let your neighbor carve for you.

—Jonathan Swift

It is very poor consolation to be told that the man who has given one a bad dinner, or poor wine, is irreproachable in private life. Even the cardinal virtues cannot atone for half-cold entrées.

—Oscar Wilde

On the Boston Tea Party:
This is the most magnificent movement of all! There is a dignity, a majesty, a sublimity, in this last effort of the patriots that I greatly admire. The people should never rise without doing something to be remembered—something notable and striking. This destruction of tea is so bold, so daring, so firm, intrepid and inflexible, and it must have so important consequences, and so lasting, that I can't but consider it as an epocha in history!

—John Adams

TEA-ED OFF

John Adams, second president of the United States, recalled the time in July 1774 when, during the early upheaval in the colonies, he was on business in Falmouth, MA. Stopping at Mrs. Huston's tavern, he asked the proprietress if "it is lawful for a weary traveler to refresh himself with a dish of tea, provided it has been honestly smuggled or paid no duties?"

Not amused by the question, Mrs. Huston replied tersely, "We have renounced all tea in this place, but I'll make you coffee."

A turning point for Adams, an ardent tea drinker, he drank Mrs. Huston's coffee and years later wrote his wife, "I have drank coffee every afternoon since, and have borne it very well."

—*Familiar Letters of John Adams and His Wife Abigail* (1876), Charles Francis Adams, ed. Boston & New York

"Take some more tea," the March Hare said to Alice, very earnestly.

"I've had nothing yet," Alice replied in an offended tone: "so I can't take more."

"You mean you can't take *less*," said the Hatter: "it's very easy to take *more* than nothing."

—Lewis Carroll (Charles Lutwidge Dodgson)

Tea to the English is really a picnic indoors.

—Alice Walker

Tea, although an Oriental,
Is a gentleman at least;
Cocoa is a cad and coward,
Cocoa is a vulgar beast.
—G.K. Chesterton

Tea! thou soft, thou sober, sage, and venerable liquid, thou female tongue-running, smile-soothing, heart-opening, wink-tippling cordial, to whose glorious insipidity I owe the happiest moments of my life, let me fall prostrate.

—Colley Cibber

Give me a platter of choice finnan haddie, freshly cooked in its bath of water and milk, add melted butter, a slice or two of hot toast, a pot of steaming Darjeeling tea, and you may tell the butler to dispense with the caviar, truffles and nightingales' tongues.

—Craig Claiborne

HIGH TEA

The First Recipe in an English Cookbook Giving Directions for Making Tea:

In these parts, we let the hot water remain too long soaking upon the Tea, which makes it extract into itself the earthy parts of the herb. The water is to remain upon the Tea, no longer than the while in which you can say the *Miserere* psalm [51] very leisurely.

—Sir Kenelm Digby, *The Closet of the Eminently Learned Sir Kenelm Digby Kt, Opened: Whereby is Discovered Several Ways of Making Metheglin, Sider, Cherry Wine, etc. Together with Excellent Directions for Cookery—also for Preserving, Conserving, Candying, etc.* (1669)

Telling a butler how to make good tea:
Warm the pot first, please, then put two heaping teaspoonfuls in the pot—
no bags—in boiling water, and when it's in, stir it. And when it comes
here, I will stir it again.

—Lynn Fontanne

**Lipton's gets into more hot water than anything.
—Advertisement for Lipton Tea™.**

Retired to tea and scandal, according to their ancient custom.

—William Congreve

Love and scandal are the best sweeteners of tea.

—Henry Fielding

On renting the essentials of life after breaking up with a lover:
I hire tea by the tea bag.

—Martin Amis

A woman is like a tea bag. It's only when she's in hot water that you
realize how strong she is.

—Nancy Reagan

Society is a strong solution of books. It draws its virtue out of what is best worth reading, as hot water draws the strength of tea leaves.

—Oliver Wendell Holmes, Sr.

Tea, though ridiculed by those who are naturally coarse in their nervous sensibilities...will always be the favourite beverage of the intellectual.

—Thomas De Quincey

In Russia a custom startling to strangers is that men drink tea in glasses and women in china cups. Here is the legend behind this custom. It seems that teacups were first made in Kronstadt, and the bottom was decorated with a view of that city. When a teahouse proprietor stinted on the tea, the picture could be seen clearly, and the customer would say to him "I can see Kronstadt." Since the proprietor could not deny this, he was caught *in flagrante delicto*. It became customary, then, for tea to be served in teahouses in glasses, at the bottom of which there was nothing to see, let alone Kronstadt!

—Alexandre Dumas

The best tea is drunk in St. Petersburg and generally throughout Russia. Since China has a common border with Siberia, tea need not be transported by water to reach Moscow or St. Petersburg. Sea voyages are very bad for tea.

—Alexandre Dumas

If you are cold, tea will warm you—if you are too heated, it will cool you—if you are depressed, it will cheer you—if you are excited it will calm you.

—William Gladstone

The pleasures of afternoon tea run like a trickle of honey through English literature from Rupert Brooke's wistful lines on the Old Vicarage at Grantchester to Miss Marple, calmly dissecting a case over tea cakes at a seaside hotel.

—Stan Hey

"Oh, for a good cup of tea!" A truly British cry that I echo so often in my travels around four o'clock in the afternoon. Tea is my panacea, my consolation—if you will, my "fix."

—Diana Kennedy

The iron kettle would be singing as it hung from its hook over the kitchen fire, the clock ticking on the wall, a white cloth spread on the table for our tea, a loaf from our weekly batch, butter from one or another of the neighboring farms marked in the pretty lozenge-shaped pattern traditional in the neighborhood, our own raspberry jam, in a ruby glass jam-dish; my glass of milk set aside from the morning on the cold slab of larder, its cream a band at the top, narrower or wider as the cow was newly calved or going dry.

—Kathleen Raine

Our trouble is that we drink too much tea. I see in this the slow revenge of the Orient, which has diverted the Yellow River down our throats.

—J.B. Priestley

Thank God for tea! What would the world do without tea?—how did it exist? I am glad I was not born before tea.

—Sydney Smith

A toast to the Cocktail Party
Where olives are speared
And friends are stabbed.
                    —anonymous

Cocktail party: A gathering held to enable forty people to talk about themselves at the same time. The man who remains after the liquor is gone is the host.

—Fred Allen

The cocktail party is a form of friendship without warmth and devotion. It is a device either for getting rid of social obligations hurriedly en masse, or for making overtures towards more serious social relationships, as in the etiquette of whoring.

—Brooks Atkinson

On cocktail parties:
A hundred standing people smiling and talking to one another, nodding like gooney birds.

—William Cole

If you happen to be unencumbered by childhood's scruples and maturity's sage ponderings, you will have gone to a great many cocktail parties in your time and will have decided, along with almost every other thing human left alive, that they are anathema. They are expensive. They are dull. They are good for a time, like a dry Martini, and like that all-demanding drink they can lift you high and then drop you hideously into a slough of boredom, morbidity, and indigestion.

—M.F.K. Fisher

RECIPE FOR TURKEY COCKTAIL

To one large turkey add one gallon of vermouth
and a demijohn of Angostura bitters. Shake.
—F. Scott Fitzgerald

The best thing about a cocktail party is being asked to it.

—Gerald Nachman

Of all so-called entertainment the cocktail party, it seems to me, has least
to be said for it. Nasty sticky little drinks taken standing, no proper conversation, nothing worthwhile to eat. Anyone that one does want to speak
to is immediately seized away by somebody else—I'd much rather stay
home and write to you.

—Rupert Hart-Davis

I misremember who first was cruel enough to nurture the cocktail party
into life. But perhaps it would be not too much to say, in fact it would be
not enough to say, that it was not worth the trouble.

—Dorothy Parker

In America, you can always find a party. In Russia, the party always finds you.

—Yakov Smirnoff

On buffets and cocktail parties:
You balance the plate between the forefinger and three other fingers, which make you a little platform, and with the forefinger and the thumb you grasp the glass and if you think that isn't hazardous, you haven't done it lately.

—Bonnie Angelo

Standing, standing, standing—why do I have to stand all the time? That is the main characteristic of social Washington.

—Daniel J. Boorstin

On a dinner party in the Kennedy White House:
The champagne was flowing like the Potomac in flood.

—Benjamin C. Bradlee

On presidential parties for the press:
[I]magine the evening from the Clintons' point of view: You are the most important man in the world. Your wife is the most important woman in the world. (At least, that's what George Stephanopoulos tells you.) And this is how you spend your evenings. Standing still for hours before a fireplace and a picture of George Washington, shaking hands and grinning for the camera, with the very people you most disdain, who are kind enough to bring to the world's attention all your little flaws.

—Maureen Dowd

Announcing the menu for a series of parties for 1,700 people attending the 1964 Democratic National Convention in Atlantic City:
Oh, my dear, it's a buffet. I have chicken à la king. I have cold turkey. I have hot rolls. I have cold ham. I have a big watermelon, all filled with fresh fruit.

—Perle Mesta

These are nice. Little Roquefort cheese morsels rolled in crushed nuts. Very tasty. Very subtle. It's the way the dry sackiness of the nuts tiptoes up against the dour savour of the cheese that is so nice, so subtle. Wonder what the Black Panthers eat here on the hors-d'oeuvre trail? Do the Panthers like little Roquefort cheese morsels rolled in crushed nuts this way, and asparagus tips in mayonnaise dabs, and meatballs petites au Coq Hardi, all of which are at the very moment being offered to them on gadrooned silver platters by maids in black uniforms with hand-ironed white aprons.

—Thomas Wolfe

Did it matter, did it matter in the least, one Prime Minister more, or less? It made no difference at this hour of the night to Mrs. Walker among the plates, saucepans, cullenders, frying-pans, chickens in aspic, ice-cream freezers, pared crusts of bread, lemons, soup tureens, and pudding basins which, however hard they washed up in the scullery seemed to be all on top of her, on the kitchen table, on chairs, while the fire blared and roared, the electric lights glared, and still supper had to be laid. All she felt was, one Prime Minister more or less made not a scrap of difference to Mrs. Walker.

—Virginia Woolf

RECIPE FOR *STUFFED DORMICE**
PERFECT FOR PARTIES

Gut and clean plump dormice, two for each guest. Make a stiff stuffing of minced pork and minced meat of other dormice. Pound this with pepper, asafoetida, pine-kernels, and *liquamen* [an ancient Roman equivalent of Worcestershire sauce]. When stuffed, sew up the mice, place in a shallow pan and cook in a slow oven.

[*Websters defines these as *any of numerous small Old World rodents.*]

—Apicius (Marcus Gavius Apicius) *The Roman Cookery Book* circa A.D. 14

You'll never get a good party going without giving things a bit of a push. It boils down to the same formula most times: good setting, good food, good drink and plenty of goodwill, as is right at this time of year.

—Michael Smith

Seating themselves on the greensward, they eat while the corks fly and there is talk, laughter and merriment, and perfect freedom, for the universe is their drawing room and the sun their lamp. Besides, they have appetite, Nature's special gift, which lends to such a meal a vivacity unknown indoors, however beautiful the surroundings.

—Brillat-Savarin

On the start of the perfect weekend:
The drink is slipping its little hand into yours.

—J. Bryan, III

> ## Now is the time for drinking, now is the time to beat the earth with unfettered foot.
> ### —Horace

On how tough Hollywood is:
I think it's a confluence of three things. There's a lot more money to be made on Wall Street. If you want real power, go to Washington. If you want sex, go into the fashion business. But if you want the whole poison cocktail in one glass, stirred up with the swizzle stick of *Hey, we're doing something creative!* go to Hollywood.

—Alec Baldwin

In a world where there is a law against people ever showing their emotions, or ever releasing themselves from the grayness of their days, a drink is not a social tool. It is a thing you need in order to live.

—Oliver Herford

A prohibitionist is the sort of man one wouldn't care to drink with—even if he drank.

—H.L. Mencken

The cocktail is a pleasant drink;
It's mild and harmless I don't think,
When you've had one you call for two,
And then you don't care what you do.
—George Ade

Whoever takes just plain ginger ale soon gets drowned out of the conversation.

—Kin Hubbard

I have very poor and unhappy brains for drinking: I could well wish courtesy would invent some other custom of entertainment.

—William Shakespeare

I drink to make other people more interesting.

—George Jean Nathan

You must be careful about giving any drink whatsoever to a bore. A lit-up bore is the worst in the world.

—David Cecil

I was enjoying myself now. I had taken two finger-bowls of Champagne, and the scene had changed before my eyes into something significant, elemental, and profound.

—F. Scott Fitzgerald

A single glass of champagne imparts a feeling of exhilaration. The nerves are braced; the imagination is stirred, the wits become more nimble.
—Winston S. Churchill

No government could survive without champagne....In the throat of our diplomatic people [it] is like oil in the wheels of an engine.
—Joseph Dargent

Champagne, if you are seeking the truth, is better than a lie detector. It encourages a man to be expansive, even reckless, while lie detectors are only a challenge to tell lies successfully.
—Graham Greene

Spoken at the moment he discovered champagne:
Come quickly, I am tasting the stars!
—Dom Pérignon

Champagne and orange juice is a great drink. The orange improves the champagne. The champagne definitely improves the orange.
—Prince Philip, Duke of Edinburgh

Champagne's funny stuff. I'm used to whiskey. Whiskey is a slap on the back, and champagne's a heavy mist before my eyes.
—James Stewart, in the movie *The Philadelphia Story*

The way I gained my title's
By a hobby which I've got
Of never letting others pay
However long the shot;
Whoever drinks at my expense
Are treated all the same,
From Dukes and Lords to cabmen down,
I make them drink Champagne.
                        —anonymous music hall song

There comes a time in every woman's life when the only thing that helps is a glass of champagne.
                        —Bette Davis, in the movie *Old Acquaintance*

I hate champagne more than anything in the world next to Seven-Up.
                        —Elaine Dundy

Champagne has the taste of an apple peeled with a steel knife.
                        —Aldous Huxley

What better way to win a heart than to spend a lazy summer afternoon in some shady and secluded country spot, a stream meandering by at the foot of a grassy slope, a few fleecy clouds floating overhead, and a bright red-and-white checkered cloth spread out, upon which sits the champagne, the fat wedge of *pâté de campagne*, the strawberries and cream?
                        —John Thorne

In praise of the martini:
When evening quickens in the street, comes a pause in the day's occupation that is known as the cocktail hour. It marks the lifeward turn. The heart wakens from coma and its dyspnea ends. Its strengthening pulse is to cross over into campground, to believe that the world has not been altogether lost or, if lost, then not altogether in vain.

—Bernard De Voto

The martini, once a symbol of American imbibing, memorialized in thousands of neon outlines of cocktail glasses, is becoming an amusing antique, like a downtown art deco apartment building.

—J.D. Reed

I am prepared to believe that a dry martini slightly impairs the palate, but think of what it does for the soul.

—Alec Waugh

This is an excellent martini—sort of tastes like it isn't there at all, just a cold cloud.

—Herman Wouk

Russians will consume marinated mushrooms and vodka, salted herring and vodka, smoked salmon and vodka, salami and vodka, caviar on brown bread and vodka, pickled cucumbers and vodka, cold tongue and vodka, red beet salad and vodka, scallions and vodka—anything and everything and vodka.

—Hedrick Smith

On drinking beer in Australia:
Beer has long been the prime lubricant in our world of social intercourse and the sacred throat-anointing fluid that accompanies the ritual of mateship. To sink a few cold ones with the blokes is both an escape and a confirmation of belonging.

—Rennie Ellis

A RECIPE FOR *CALF'S HEAD CHEESE*

Boil a calf's head in water enough to cover it [put the head into boiling water and let it remain about five minutes; hold it by the ear, and with the back of the knife scrape off the hair (should it not come off easily dip the head again in boiling water)], until the meat leaves the bones; then take it with a skimmer into a wooden bowl or tray; take from it every particle of bone; chop it small; season with pepper and salt,...add a tablespoon of finely chopped sweet herbs; lay in a cloth in a colander, put the minced meat into it, then fold the cloth over it, lay a plate over, and on it a gentle weight. When cold it may be sliced thin for supper or sandwiches.   Spread each slice with made mustard.

—Hugo Ziemann, Steward of the White House, and Mrs. F.L. Gillette, *The Original White House Cookbook: Contains Cooking, Toilet and Household Recipes, Menus, Dinner-giving, Table Etiquette, Care of the Sick, Health Suggestions, Facts Worth Knowing, etc.* (1887)

Give me books, fruit, French wine, fine weather and a little music out of doors, played by somebody I do not know.

—John Keats

A beatific smile spread over his face! Man had tasted the oyster!

In half an hour, mankind was plunging into the waves searching for oysters. The oyster's doom was sealed. His monstrous pretension that he belonged in the van of evolutionary progress was killed forever. He had been tasted, and found food. He would never again battle for supremacy. Meekly he yielded to his fate. He is food to this day.

—Don Marquis

Oysters: Nobody eats them anymore: too expensive.

—Gustave Flaubert

Actually in our present conditions of life the thing without price would seem to be more the oyster, if it were a good one, than the pearl, the quality of fake jewelry having risen in exactly inverse proportion to that of real seafood.

—Eleanor Clark

See that bivalve social climber
Feeding the rich Mrs. Hoggenheimer,
Think of his joy as he gaily glides
Down to the middle of her gilded insides.
Proud little oyster.

—Cole Porter

Beneficent Oyster, good to taste, good for the stomach and the soul, grant us the blessing of your further mystery.

—Eleanor Clark

"But wait a bit," the Oysters cried,
"Before we have our chat.
For some of us are out of breath,
And all of us are fat!"

—Lewis Carroll

In general, only mute things are eaten alive—plants and invertebrates. If oysters shrieked as they were pried open, or squealed when jabbed with a fork, I doubt whether they would be eaten alive. But as it is, thoughtful people quite callously look for the muscular twitch as they drop lemon juice on a poor oyster, to be sure that it is alive before they eat it.

—Marston Bates

I never was much of an oyster eater, nor can I relish them *in naturalibus* as some do, but require a quantity of sauces, lemons, cayenne peppers, bread and butter, and so forth, to render them palatable.

—William M. Thackeray

An oyster, that marvel of delicacy, that concentration of sapid excellence, that mouthful before all other mouthfuls, who first had faith to believe in it, and courage to execute? The exterior is not persuasive.

—Henry Ward Beecher

He was a very valiant man who first adventured on eating oysters.
—Thomas Fuller

He had often eaten oysters, but had never had enough.
—W.S. Gilbert

Oyster dear to the gourmet, beneficent Oyster, exciting rather than sating, all stomachs digest you, all stomachs bless you.
—Seneca

A RECIPE FOR *FRESSE CRABBE BAKE*

Take a crabbe, breke hym a- sonder into a dysshe, then make ye shell clene. Put in the crabbe- mete agane, tempre it with vynegre & pouder, than cover it with brede, and sende it to the kytchyn to hete. Set it before your lourde, and breke the grete clawes, and laye them in a disshe.
—Wynkyn de Worde, *The Boke of Kervynge* (1508; The second oldest known cookbook printed in English. Several new editions were published through 1613 attesting to its popularity.)

Oysters are not really food, but are relished to bully the sated stomach into further eating.

—Seneca

On caviar:
The roe of the Russian sturgeon has probably been present at more important international affairs than have all the Russian dignitaries of history combined. This seemingly simple article of diet has taken its place in the world along with pearls, sables, old silver, and Cellini cups.

—James Beard

Caviar is to dining what a sable coat is to a girl in an evening dress.

—Ludwig Bemelmans

There is more simplicity in the man who eats caviar on impulse than in the man who eats grape-nuts on principle.

—G.K. Chesterton

Under cover of the clinking of water goblets and silverware and bone china, I paved my plate with chicken slices. Then I covered the chicken slices with caviar thickly as if I were spreading peanut butter on a piece of bread. Then I picked up the chicken slices in my fingers one by one, rolled them so the caviar wouldn't ooze off and ate them.

—Sylvia Plath

It wasn't until 1707 that [the company name] settled down into Fortnum, collected its Mason and became the sweetest sound in the English language for those countless perceptive thousands who know that life can be sustained by bread and water, but it is given a sharp, upward boost by the more imaginative combination of caviar and champagne.

—Fortnum & Mason, from *The Delectable History of Fortnum & Mason*

Cockroaches and socialites are the only things that can stay up all night and eat anything.

—Herb Caen

Popcorn [is] the sentimental good-time Charlie of American foods.

—Patricia Linden

Today, millions of Americans who sit munching popcorn before flickering movie screens, television sets, and fireplaces are following an ancient tradition. Throughout much of the hemisphere generations of Indians popped corn in earthen vessels and ate it around open fires. One-thousand-year-old specimens of the grain from ancient, musty Peruvian tombs still popped when heated!

—Nicholas P. Hardeman

Pesto is the quiche of the '80s.

—Nora Ephron

Real men don't eat quiche.

—Bruce Feirstein

The Moon Pie is a bedrock of the country store and a rural tradition. It is more than a snack. It is a cultural artifact.

—William Ferris

Chicken salad has a certain glamour about it. Like the little black dress, it is chic and adaptable anywhere.

—Laurie Colwin

ABOUT *SWEETBREADS*...

There are two in a calf, which are considered delicacies. Select the largest. The color should be clear and a shade darker than the fat. Before cooking in any manner let them lie for a half an hour in tepid water; then throw it into hot water to whiten and harden, after which draw off the outer casing, remove the little pipes, and cut into thin slices. They should always be thoroughly cooked.

    —Hugo Ziemann, Steward of the White House, and Mrs. F.L. Gillette, *The Original White House Cookbook: Contains Cooking, Toilet and Household Recipes, Menus, Dinner-giving, Table Etiquette, Care of the Sick, Health Suggestions, Facts Worth Knowing, etc.* (1887)

Last night I dreamed I ate a ten-pound marshmallow, and when I woke up the pillow was gone.

—Tommy Cooper

There is a charm in improvised eating which a regular meal lacks, and there was a glamour never to be recaptured in secret picnics on long sunny mornings on the roof of the Hall....I would sit up there with my cousin Tooter, consuming sweets bought with our weekly pocket money and discussing possible futures....The sweets I remember best were white and tubular, much thinner than any cigarette, filled with a dark chocolate filling. If I found one now I am sure it would have the taste of hope.

—Graham Greene

When the cold came before the snow, we went skating on Williams Lake across the Arm. Remembering her own childhood, my mother put hot baked potatoes in the boots of our skates. After the rowboat ferry ride, one oar almost touching the edge of the ice line on the half-frozen Arm, and the walk up to the lake, the skates were warm to put on and the potatoes cool enough to eat.

—Robert MacNeil

My idea of heaven is eating *pâtés de foie gras* to the sound of trumpets.

—Sydney Smith

I hate television. I hate it as much as peanuts. But I can't stop eating peanuts.

—Orson Welles

DINNER

During the whole repast, the general conversation was upon eating. Every dish was discussed, and the antiquities of every bottle of wine supplied with the most eloquent annotations. Talleyrand himself analyzed the dinner with as much interest and seriousness as if he had been discussing some political question of importance.

—Lady Frances Shelley

WHEN EATING, JUST EAT

Formal dinners, especially the types graced by political luminaries of the day, depend heavily upon the quality and quantity of the conversation as well as the food. Imagine then the despair of Washingtonian hostesses in planning such parties when Calvin ("Silent Cal") Coolidge was on the guest list.

One such hostess thought she had found the answer to her prayers. She sat the then Vice President of the United States next to the effervescent and brilliant daughter of former President Teddy Roosevelt, but even the sparkling Alice Roosevelt Longworth was overtaxed in trying to evoke a conversation with the stoic Coolidge.

Finally, toward the end of dinner, a perturbed and exasperated Mrs. Longworth said, with more than a hint of ire, "You go to so many dinners. You must get terribly bored."

Unflapped and true to form, Coolidge replied, "Well, a man must eat."

Dinner was made for eatin', not for talkin'.

—William M. Thackeray

When I complained of having dined at a splendid table without hearing one sentence of conversation worthy of being remembered, Doctor Johnson said, "Sir, there seldom is any such conversation."

Boswell: "Why then meet at table?"

Johnson: "Why, to eat and drink together, and to promote kindness; and, sir, this is better done when there is no solid conversation; for when there is, people differ in opinion, and get into bad humor, or some of the company who are not capable of any such conversation, are left out, and feel themselves uneasy. It was for this reason, Sir Robert Walpole said, he always talked bawdy at his table, because in that all could join."

—James Boswell

Sir, respect your dinner: idolize it, enjoy it properly. You will be many hours in the week, many weeks in the year, and many years in your life happier if you do.

—William M. Thackeray

A man's own dinner is to himself so important that he cannot bring himself to believe that it is a matter utterly indifferent to anyone else.

—Anthony Trollope

A man who can dominate a London dinner table can dominate the world.

—Oscar Wilde

The art of dining well is no slight art, the pleasure not a slight pleasure.
—Michel de Montaigne

A man seldom thinks with more earnestness of anything than he does of his dinner.

—Samuel Johnson

Among the great whom Heaven has made to shine,
How few have learned the art of arts,—to dine!
—Oliver Wendell Holmes, Sr.

Music with dinner is an insult both to the cook and the violinist.
—G.K. Chesterton

Light the candles and pour the red wine into your glass. Before you begin to eat, raise your glass in honor of yourself. The company is the best you'll ever have.

—Daniel Halpern

Oh, the pleasure of eating my dinner alone!

—Charles Lamb

In response to the servant who had prepared only a simple meal when Lucullus was dining alone:
What, did you not know, then, that today Lucullus dines with Lucullus?
—Lucullus

What you seek in vain for, half your life, one day you come full upon, all the family at dinner.

—Henry David Thoreau

Strange to see how a good dinner and feasting reconciles everybody.

—Samuel Pepys

> *After a good dinner, one can forgive anybody, even one's own relations.*
> *—Oscar Wilde*

When my mother had to get dinner for eight she'd just make enough for 16 and only serve half.

—Gracie Allen

The most remarkable thing about my mother is that for thirty years she served the family nothing but leftovers. The original meal has never been found.

—Calvin Trillin

A warmed-up dinner was never worth much.

—Boileau

A man is in general better pleased when he has a good dinner upon the table than when his wife talks Greek.

—Samuel Johnson

Everything ends this way in France, everything. Weddings, christenings, duels, burials, swindlings, diplomatic affairs—everything is a pretext for a good dinner.

—Jean Anouilh

Americans are just beginning to regard food the way the French always have. Dinner is not what you do in the evening before something else. Dinner is the evening.

—Art Buchwald

Dining is the privilege of civilisation....The nation which knows how to dine has learnt the leading lesson of progress. It implies both the will and the skill to reduce to order, and surround with idealisms and graces, the more material conditions of human existence; and wherever that will and that skill exist, life cannot be wholly ignoble.

—Mrs. Isabella Beeton

A rich soup; a small turbot; a saddle of venison; an apricot tart: this is a dinner fit for a king.

—Brillat-Savarin

There is a universe between the meal set brusquely before you and that on which thought and careful planning have been spent.

—Edward Bunyard

When compelled to cook, I produce a meal that would make a sword swallower gag.

—Russell Baker

That all-softening, overpowering knell,
The tocsin of the soul—the dinner bell.
—Lord Byron

A two-pound turkey and a fifty-pound cranberry—that's Thanksgiving dinner at Three-Mile Island.

—Johnny Carson

In a house where there is plenty, supper is soon cooked.

—Cervantes

All people are made alike.
They are made of bones, flesh and dinners.
Only the dinners are different.
—Gertrude Louise Cheney
(Written by the author at age nine.)

A simple dinner in a poor man's house, without tapestries and purple, has smoothed the wrinkles from the anxious brow.

—Horace

Found a little patched-up inn in the village of Bulson....Proprietor had nothing but potatoes; but what a feast he laid before me. Served them in five different courses—potato soup, potato fricassee, potatoes creamed, potato salad and finished with potato pie. It may be because I had not eaten for 36 hours, but that meal seems about the best I ever had.

—Douglas MacArthur

The last dinner of each month, when money simply was not there to be stretched, called for a favorite of my grandmother: hot lemon tea served with a variety of olives called *throumbes*... and brown bread.

—Rena Salaman

They make their pride in making their dinner cost much; I make my pride in making my dinner cost little.

—Henry David Thoreau

Sunday supper (when the preacher from the church down the road would often stop by) was a celebration. Food was the guest of honor, covering so much of the table there was hardly room for plates.

—Oprah Winfrey

On her "humble" Washington dinner parties:
With my little dinners I like to feel I am helping to save Western civilization.

—Gwen Cafritz

Disguise it as you will, flavor it as you will, call it what you will, umble-pie is umble-pie, and nothing else.

—James Russell Lowell

UMBLE* PIE

Cut the Umbles in small pieces, and cut fat Bacon in small pieces. Mix them together, and season them with Salt, Pepper, and Nutmeg. Strip some Thyme, and mince some Lemon, and mix them; you may lay Suet minced in the bottom.

Fill your Pastry, cover them with thin Slices of Bacon, and a good Quantity of Butter. Let it be well soaked in the Oven, and when it is bak'd, beat up Butter with Claret, Lemon, and stript Thyme.

Pour it into your Pastry and serve it up hot.

[*What has come down to us as the expression, "Eating humble pie" really began as umble pie, the umbles being the least desirable bits of offal left over from whatever game was currently gracing the larder. These were scraps of the liver, lungs, and other viscera remaining from the slaughter of the animals. Needless to say, eating umble pie, especially knowing that it was made of the stuff animal feed was made of, could be a humbling experience— it was hardly a pie offered to society's upper crust.]

—John Nott, *The Cook's and Confectioner's Dictionary; or, the Accomplished Housewife's Companion* (1723)

111

Summer has an unfortunate effect upon hostesses who have been unduly influenced by the photography of Irving Penn and take the season as a cue to serve dinners of astonishingly meager proportions. These they call light, a quality which, while most welcome in comedies, cotton shirts and hearts, is not an appropriate touch at dinner.

—Fran Lebowitz

One glance at her and I knew at once the sort of things that Dorcas would cook, that Dorcas was born to cook. Never, in later life, have I sat down to dinner without saying to myself, "Ah! things look Dorcassy tonight!" or, "Alas! there is nothing Dorcassy here."

—Don Marquis

Dr. Middleton misdoubted the future as well as the past of the man who did not, in becoming gravity, exult to dine. That man he deemed unfit for this world and the next.

—George Meredith

Dinner...Possessed only two dramatic features—the wine was a farce and the food a tragedy.

—Anthony Poole

I do not think that anything serious should be done after dinner, as nothing should be before breakfast.

—George Saintsbury

Though we eat little flesh and drink no wine,
Yet let's be merry; we'll have tea and toast;
Custards for supper, and an endless host
Of syllabubs and jellies and mince-pies,
And other such lady-like luxuries.
—Percy Bysshe Shelley

Serenely full, the epicure would say,
"Fate cannot harm me, I have dined to-day."
—Sydney Smith

Bilbo Baggins to the trolls who plan to eat him:
And please don't cook me, kind sirs! I am a good cook myself, and cook better than I cook, if you see what I mean. I'll cook beautifully for you, a perfectly beautiful breakfast for you, if only you won't have me for supper.
—J.R.R. Tolkien

One cannot think well, love well, sleep well, if one has not dined well.
—Virginia Woolf

Dining is and always was a great artistic opportunity.
—Frank Lloyd Wright

No dish changes quite so much from season to season as soup. Summer's soups come chilled, in pastel colors strewn with herbs. If hot they are sheer, insubstantial broths afloat with seafood. In winter they turn steaming and thick to serve with slabs of rustic, crusty bread.

—Florence Fabricant

Too many cooks spoil the broth.

—Sir Balthazar Gerbier

What comforted me? That is easy. It was a strong cold chicken jelly so very, very thick. My Mother's Chinese cook would fix it. He would cook it down, condense it—this broth with all sorts of feet in it, then it would gell into sheer bliss. It kept me alive once for three weeks when I was ill as a child. And I've always craved it since.

—James Beard

Onion soup sustains. The process of making it is somewhat like the process of learning to love. It requires commitment, extraordinary effort, time, and will make you cry.

—Ronni Lundy

Some cooks use the flesh of chickens and pigs for one soup, and as chickens and pigs have souls, they will hold these cooks to account, in the next world, for their treatment of them in this.

—Yuan Mei

My good health is due to a soup made of white doves. It is simply wonderful as a tonic.

—Mme. Chiang Kai-shek

No. I don't take soup. You can't build a meal on a lake.

—Elsie de Wolfe (Lady Mendl)

Do not make loon soup.

—*The Eskimo Cookbook* (1957)

A RECIPE FOR *SOUP TO GO*

First prepare the soup of your choice and pour it into a bowl. Then, take the bowl and quickly turn it upside down on the cookie tray. Lift the bowl ever so gently so that the soup retains the shape of the bowl. *Gently* is the key word here. Then, with the knife cut the soup down the middle into halves, then quarters, and *gently* reassemble the soup into a cube. Some of the soup will run off into the cookie tray. Lift this soup up by the corners and fold slowly into a cylindrical soup staff. Place the packet in your purse or inside coat pocket, and pack off to work.

—Steve Martin

On being served matzo ball soup three meals in a row:
Isn't there any other part of the matzo you can eat?

—Marilyn Monroe

Chicken Stock is one of those necessary and comforting fluids.

—Jeff Smith (The Frugal Gourmet)

AN "ECONOMICAL" RECIPE FOR ASPARAGUS SOOP

Take twelve pounds of lean beef, cut in slices; then put a quarter of a pound of butter in a stew pan over the fire, and put your beef in.

Let it boil up quick until it begins to brown; then put in a pint of brown ale, and a gallon of water, and cover it close. Let it stew gently for an hour and a half. Put in what spice you like in the stewing, and strain off the liquor, and scum off all the fat. Then put in some vermicelly, and some sallery wash'd and cut small, half a hundred of Asparagus cut small, and potatoes boiled tender and cut. Put all these in and let them boil gently till tender.

Just as 'tis going up, fry a handful of spinage in butter, and throw in a French roll.

[No mention is made of how many family members would be fed by this "economical" recipe.]

—Elizabeth Smith, *The Complete Housewife; or, Accomplish'd Gentlewoman's Companion* (1727)

The potato and leek soup that is prepared night after night in the kitchens of nearly every Parisian *concierge* and in the kitchens of nearly every Île de France working family is nothing more than potatoes and leeks more or less finely sliced or cut up, depending on the *bonne femme*, boiled in salted water, and served, a piece of butter being either added then to the soup or being put to join the inevitable crust of bread in the soup plate before the boiled vegetables are poured over. It carries within it always the message of well-being and, were my vice and my curiosity more restrained, I, too, would adore to eat it every evening of my life.

—Richard Olney

Soup and fish explain half of the emotions of life.

—Sydney Smith

Hors d'oeuvres have always a pathetic interest for me: they remind me of one's childhood that one goes through, wondering what the next course is going to be like—and during the rest of the menu one wishes one had eaten more of the hors d'oeuvres.

—Saki (H.H. Munro)

If I can't have too many truffles, I'll do without truffles.

—Colette

Your truffles must come to the table in their own stock....And as you break open this jewel sprung from a poverty-stricken soil, imagine—if you have never visited it—the desolate kingdom where it rules. For it kills the dog rose, drains life from the oak, ripens beneath an ungrateful bed of pebbles.

—Colette

I prefer my oysters fried;
That way I know my oysters died.

—Roy G. Blount, Jr.

I will not eat oysters. I want my food dead—not sick, not wounded—dead.

—Woody Allen

If you don't love life you can't enjoy an oyster; there is a shock of freshness to it and intimations of the ages of man, some piercing intuition of the sea and all its weeds and breezes.

—Eleanor Clark

A snail is just a walking intestine.

—Georges Auer

I sometimes feel that more lousy dishes are presented under the banner of pâté than any other.

—Kingsley Amis

Describing the pâté at London's Simpson's-on-the-Strand restaurant:
It scored right away with me by being the smooth, fine-grained sort, not the coarse flaky, dry-on-the-outside rubbish full of chunks of gut and gristle to testify to its authenticity.

—Kingsley Amis

A pâté is nothing more than French meat loaf that's had a couple of cocktails.

—Carol Cutler

On the proper salad:
It freshens without enfeebling and fortifies without irritating.

—Brillat-Savarin

President Johnson preferred his salad chopped so fine that he could eat it with a spoon. He was a very rapid eater.

—Henry Haller

Catholicism has changed tremendously in recent years. Now when Communion is served there is also a salad bar.

—Bill Maher

Lettuce is divine, although I'm not sure it's really a food.

—Diana Vreeland

CHEF SALAD

The original Chef's Salad was the creation of Chef Louis Diat in the early 1900s during his reign as head chef of New York's famous Ritz-Carlton Hotel. As a precursor of today's dumping ground for cold cuts and leftovers, Chef Diat's recipe included watercress and the ever-popular smoked ox tongue.

Better is a dinner of herbs where love is, than a stalled ox and hatred therewith.

—The Bible

Newman's Own salad dressing: The star of oil and vinegar and the oil and vinegar of the stars.

—Paul Newman

On being a Mafia cook:
I was enticed to join another club on a sort of double-secret probation. This club was called the Full-Blooded Italians, or, for short, FBI. The guys in my new club asked me to spy on the guys in my old club [the Mothers And Fathers Italian Association, or MAFIA] who had tried to kill me. I had no problem with that. Revenge, like my Cicoria Insalata, is best eaten cold.

—Joseph (Joe Dogs) Iannuzzi

"It is an art too seldom met with," Adam declared, "the correct slicing of cucumber. In Victorian times there was—I believe—an implement or device for that purpose."

—Barbara Pym

'Tis not *her* coldness, father,
That chills my labouring breast;
It's that confounded cucumber
I've ate and can't digest.
—R.H. Barham

A cucumber should be well sliced, and dressed with pepper and vinegar, and then thrown out, as good for nothing.

—Samuel Johnson

The cherry tomato is a marvelous invention, producing as it does a satisfactorily explosive squish when bitten.

—Judith Martin (Miss Manners)

Just when you're beginning to think pretty well of people, you run across somebody who puts sugar on sliced tomatoes.

—Will Cuppy

An honest laborious Country-man, with good Bread, Salt and a little Parsley, will make a contented meal with a roasted Onion.

—John Evelyn

SALAD BOWL POLITICS

Although a man of few words, U.S. President Calvin Coolidge was also known for getting in the last word. Back in New England with his wife and in retirement, the ex-President was talking politics with friends over lunch. Specifically, the debate was over United States recognition of the Soviet Union. As the tenor became more heated than friendly, Mrs. Coolidge tried to switch the conversation to food, asking all seated if they preferred French or Russian dressing for their salads. Calvin Coolidge replied tersely, "I'll take the one that isn't red."

There is in every cook's opinion
No savoury dish without an onion:
But lest your kissing should be spoiled
The onion must be thoroughly boiled.
—Jonathan Swift

The kitchen, reasonably enough, was the scene of my first gastronomic adventure. I was on all fours. I crawled into the vegetable bin, settled on a giant onion and ate it, skin and all. It must have marked me for life, for I have never ceased to love the hearty flavor of raw onions.

—James Beard

Let onion atoms dwell within the bowl,
And, scarce suspected, animate the whole.
—Sydney Smith

Potherbs in the autumn garden round the house
Of my friend the hermit behind his rough-cut
Timber gate. I never wrote and asked for them
But he's sent this basket full of Winter Onions, still
Damp with dew. Delicately grass-green bundles,
White jade small bulbs.
Chill threatens an old man's innards,
These will warm and comfort me.

—Tu Fu

"What are poireaux?"

"Leeks."

"It looks like long, green, quite big onions," young Tom said. "Only it's not bright shiny like onions. It's dull shiny. The leaves are green and the ends are white. You boil it and eat it cold with olive oil and vinegar mixed with salt and pepper. You eat the whole thing, top and all. It's delicious. I believe I've eaten as much of it as maybe anyone in the world."

—Ernest Hemingway

I say it's spinach, and I say the hell with it.
—E.B. White

Like warmed-up cabbage served at each repast,
The repetition kills the wretch at last.

—Juvenal

Cabbage: A...vegetable about as large and wise as a man's head.

—Ambrose Bierce

It is quite affecting to observe how much the olive tree is to the country people. Its fruit supplies them with food, medicine and light; its leaves, winter fodder for the goats and sheep; it is their shelter from the heat and its branches and roots supply them with firewood. The olive tree is the peasant's all in all.

—Frederica Bremer

On olives:
The whole Mediterranean, the sculpture, the palms, the gold breads, the bearded heroes, the wine, the ideas, the ships, the moonlight, the winged gorgons, the bronze men, the philosophers—all of it seems to rise in the sour, pungent smell of these black olives between the teeth. A taste older than meat, older than wine. A taste as old as cold water.

—Lawrence Durrell

Eggplant is a handsome vegetable indeed, with its green cap and purple skin.

—Julia Child

Cogito ergo spud. I think, therefore I yam.

—Herb Caen

A potato is a tuber, but the fact should be left in the decent obscurity of agricultural textbooks.

—H.W. Fowler

On his role as founder of the Potato Museum in Washington, DC:
We're serious but not solemn about potatoes here. The potato has lots of eyes, but no mouth. That's where I come in.

—E. Thomas Hughes

Sex is good, but not as good as fresh sweet corn.

—Garrison Keillor

Hunger maketh hard beans sweet.

—John Heywood

Inhabitants of underdeveloped nations and victims of natural disasters are the only people who have ever been happy to see soybeans.

—Fran Lebowitz

If pale beans bubble for you in a red earthenware pot
You can oft decline the dinners of sumptuous hosts.

—Martial

Eating an artichoke is like getting to know someone really well.

—Willi Hastings

Within every artichoke is an acanthus leaf, and the acanthus is what man would have made of the artichoke, had God asked him his advice.

—André Malraux

Please understand the reason why Chinese vegetables taste so good. It is simple. The Chinese do not cook them, they just threaten them!

—Jeff Smith (The Frugal Gourmet)

Bamboo-shoots ought never to be cut with a knife which has just been used on onions.

—Yuan Mei

The best of all sauces is hunger engendered by exercise in the open air, and, equally, the best of digestives is pleasant company.

—Saint Ange

Closing for his letters:
Red beans and ricely yours,

—Louis Armstrong

Making love without love is like trying to make a soufflé without egg whites.

—Simone Beck

On béarnaise sauce:
It frightens me! With it one might never stop eating. Merely reading the recipe arouses my hunger.

—Baron Brisse

This curry was like a performance of Beethoven's Ninth Symphony that I'd once heard played on a player and amplifier built by personnel of the Royal Electrical and Mechanical Engineers, especially the last movement, with everything screaming and banging "Joy." It stunned, it made one fear great art. My father could say nothing after the meal.

—Anthony Burgess

The best sauce in the world is hunger.

—Cervantes

Woe to the cook whose sauce has no sting.

—Geoffrey Chaucer

> But since he stood for England
> And knew what England means,
> Unless you give him bacon
> You must not give him beans.
> —G.K. Chesterton

AND THAT'S THE WAY IT WAS...

Henry Haller became Executive Chef to the White House during the Johnson administration. Imagine the butterflies he must have felt when, on a night shortly after assuming this position, he tuned in to watch Walter Cronkite on the *CBS Evening News* and heard the following report:

"We have been unable to determine if the new chef has passed the test on chili con carne. If he has used ground round steak, as Mrs. Eisenhower used to do, that news would be automatically suppressed in the interests of public order in Texas. If he learns to use chuck meat, on the lean side and from an old critter, he can expect a long and happy life in the White House kitchen".

A TEXAS RECIPE FOR CHILI

Put a pot of chili on the stove to simmer.
Let it simmer. Meanwhile, broil a good steak.
Eat the steak. Let the chili simmer. Ignore it.
—Gov. Allan Shivers of Texas

The aroma of good chili should generate rapture akin to a lover's kiss.
—The Chili Appreciation Society International, motto

Chili lovers come from every walk of life. Chili attracts truck drivers, celebrities, doctors, lawyers, and schoolteachers. Rich and poor undergo a Jekyll/Hyde-like transformation and mild-mannered pillars of the community show no mercy when the topic of conversation turns to controversial chili.
—Jane Butel

Chili is not so much food as a state of mind. Addictions to it are formed early in life and the victims never recover. On blue days in October I get this passionate yearning for a bowl of chili, and I nearly lose my mind.
—Margaret Cousins

Chili is much improved by having had a day to contemplate its fate.

—John Steele Gordon

Next to jazz music, there is nothing that lifts the spirit and strengthens the soul more than a good bowl of chili.

—Harry James

Describing Texas chili:
The bowl of blessedness!

—Will Rogers

The quarreling that has gone on for generations over New England clam chowder versus Manhattan clam chowder (the Maine legislature once passed a law outlawing the mixing of tomatoes with clams) is but a minor spat alongside the raging feuds that have arisen out of chili recipes.

—Martina and William Neely

What I love about cooking is that after a hard day, there is something comforting about the fact that if you melt butter and add flour and then hot stock, *it will get thick!* It's a sure thing! It's a sure thing in a world where nothing is sure; it has a mathematical certainty in a world where those of us who long for some kind of certainty are forced to settle for crossword puzzles.

—Nora Ephron

Every cook commends his own sauce.

—Sir Balthazar Gerbier

On picking mushrooms:
You never know unless you *know* you know.

—Jay Jacobs

Finding a strange, slimy, luminous colored growth on dark rotting wood is surprise and pleasure; to extend that experience into identifying it and eating it is even better.

—*The Whole Earth Catalog*

Life is too short to stuff a mushroom.

—Storm Jameson

Dennis the Menace: No more turkey, but I'd like some more of the bread it ate.

—Hank Ketcham

It is the sauce that distinguishes a good chef. The *saucier* is a soloist in the orchestra of a great kitchen.

—Fernand Point

Madam, I have been looking for a person who disliked gravy all my life: let us swear eternal friendship.

—Sydney Smith

What is sauce for the goose may be sauce for the gander, but it is not necessarily sauce for the chicken, the duck, the turkey or the Guinea hen.

—Alice B. Toklas

To Make Fairy Butter

Take the Yolks of two hard Eggs, and beat them in a Marble Mortar with a large Spoonful of Orange-flower water and two Tea Spoonfuls of fine Sugar beat to Powder.

Beat this all together till it is fine Paste, then mix it up with about as much fresh Butter out of the Churn and force it through a fine strainer full of little holes into a Plate. This is a pretty thing to set off a Table at Supper.

—Mrs. Hannah Glasse, *The Art of Cookery made Plain and Easy* (1747; First cookbook written in English by a woman to have achieved any notoriety—was a bestseller in Great Britain for almost 100 years.)

A sauce, in other words, adds something, really two things: a taste as well as the opportunity to think about how the thing was made. This is the same kind of pleasure we derive when we look at a painting; the eye is pleased, while the mind explores the esthetic windings of a technique and a willed structure.

—Raymond Sokolov

Chutney is marvelous. I'm mad about it. To me, it's very imperial.

—Diana Vreeland

Acorns were good until bread was found.

—Francis Bacon

From a Russian café sign:
Bread is the warmest, kindest of words. Write it always with a capital letter, like your own name.

—anonymous

> Back of the loaf is the snowy flour,
> And back of the flour the mill,
> And back of the mill is the wheat and the shower
> And the sun and the Father's will.

—Maltbie D. Babcock

The sky is the daily bread of the eyes.

—Ralph Waldo Emerson

Man does not live by bread alone.

—The Bible

Man is a creature who lives not upon bread alone, but principally by catch-words.

—Robert Louis Stevenson

Bread is the king of the table and all else is merely the court that surround the king. The countries are the soup, the meat, the vegetables, the salad...but bread is king.

—Louis Bromfield

Give us this day our daily bread.
—The Bible

The history of man from the beginning has been the history of his struggle for his daily bread.

—Josue de Castro

Without bread all is misery.

—William Cobbett

God made yeast, as well as dough, and loves fermentation just as dearly as he loves vegetation.

—Ralph Waldo Emerson

Honest bread is very well—it's the butter that makes the temptation.
—Douglas Jerrold

They that have no other meat,
Bread and butter are glad to eat.
—Thomas Fuller

Winnie the Pooh:
I do like a bit of butter to my bread.

—A.A. Milne

Open thine eyes, and thou shalt be satisfied with bread.
—The Bible

A loaf of bread, the Walrus said,
Is what we chiefly need:
Pepper and vinegar besides
Are very good indeed.
—Lewis Carroll (Charles Lutwidge Dodgson)

I know which side my bread is buttered.

—John Heywood

His bread is buttered on both sides.

—Thomas Fuller

And the Quangle Wangle said
To himself on the crumpety tree
"Jam and Jelly and bread
are the best foods for me."
—Edward Lear

Here is bread, which strengthens man's heart, and therefore is called the staff of life.

—Matthew Henry

O God! that bread should be so dear,
And flesh and blood so cheap!
—Thomas Hood

Reporting on the trial of a collective farm manager in the U.S.S.R. charged with feeding bread to pigs:
In the phrases of songs and poems...bread is gold, it is the motherland, it is the hard work of the masses, it is life itself.

—Seth Mydans

Bread is like dresses, hats and shoes—in other words, essential!

—Emily Post

What bread men break is broke to them again.

—John Taylor (The Water Poet)

Better to have bread and an onion with peace than stuffed fowl with strife.
—Arab Proverb

My piece of bread only belongs to me when I know that everyone else has a share, and that no one starves while I eat.
—Leo Tolstoy

Cast thy bread upon the waters: for thou shalt find it after many days.
—The Bible

Bread deals with living things, with giving life, with growth, with the seed, the grain that nurtures. It is not coincidence that we say bread is the staff of life.
—Lionel Poilane

For a few days or a week or a fortnight, the fields stood "ripe unto harvest." It was the one perfect period in the hamlet year. The human eye loves to rest upon wide expanses of pure colour: the moors in the purple heyday of the heather, miles of green downland, and the sea when it lies calm and blue and boundless, all delight it; but to some none of these, lovely as they are, can give the same satisfaction of spirit as acres upon acres of golden corn. *There* is both beauty and bread and the seeds of bread for future generations.
—Flora Thompson

ABOUT BREAD...

Among all civilized people bread has become an article of food of the first necessity; and properly so, for it constitutes of itself a complete life sustainer...combining the sustaining powers of the animal and vegetable kingdoms in one product. As there is no one article of food that enters so largely into our daily fare as bread, so no degree of skill in preparing other articles can compensate for lack of knowledge in the art of making good, palatable and nutritious bread.

—Hugo Ziemann, Steward of the White House, and Mrs. F.L. Gillette, *The Original White House Cookbook: Contains Cooking, Toilet and Household Recipes, Menus, Dinner-giving, Table Etiquette, Care of the Sick, Health Suggestions, Facts Worth Knowing, etc.* (1887)

It is better to have loafed and lost than never to have loafed at all.

—James Thurber

Nothin' says lovin' like somethin' from the oven.®

—Advertisement for Pillsbury™ foods and baking products

What hymns are sung.
What praises said.
For homemade miracles of bread?
—Louis Untermeyer

One remembers flavor more than dates and times in the memory portion of the brain. Taste and smell and grandma's rolling the dough...that's it!
—Jeff Smith (The Frugal Gourmet)

The smell of good bread baking, like the sound of lightly flowing water, is indescribable in its evocation of innocence and delight.
—M.F.K. Fisher

Raising children is like making biscuits: it is as easy to raise a big batch as one, while you have your hands in the dough.
—E.W. Howe

I am going to learn how to make bread to-morrow. So you may imagine me with my sleeves rolled up, mixing flour, milk, saleratus, etc., with a deal of grace. I advise that if you don't know how to make the staff of life to learn with dispatch.
—Emily Dickinson

I learned to bake wonderful bread—I had always thought of bread as something that just happened, but Bermuda bread was so horrible I bought some yeast and a cook book and had hot rolls for breakfast, and loaf bread for my tea.
—Katherine Anne Porter

On opening a large bakery:
The problem was I had no idea how to bake bread! I kind of worked backward—I opened a bakery and then learned to bake.

—Nancy Silverton

On shopping for bread in New York City:
Do you know on this one block you can buy croissants in five different places? There's one store called Bonjour Croissant. It makes me want to go to Paris and open a store called Hello Toast.

—Fran Lebowitz

Toast was a big item in my mother's culinary pharmacopeia. At first it was served plain and dry, but that was soon followed by crisp, sweet cinnamon toast, then baby-bland toast that tasted soothingly of fresh air. Thick slices of French toast, crisp and golden outside but moist and eggy within, would probably come next, always topped with a melting knob of sweet butter and a dusting of confectioner's sugar. I knew I was close to recovery when I got the toast I liked best—almost-burned rye bread toast covered with salt butter.

—Mimi Sheraton

The smell of buttered toast simply talked to Toad, and with no uncertain voice; talked of warm kitchens, of breakfasts on bright frosty mornings, of cosy parlour firesides on winter evenings, when one's ramble was over and slippered feet were propped on the fender; of the purring of contented cats, and twitter of sleepy canaries.

—Kenneth Grahame

My family dumplings are sleek and seductive, yet stout and masculine. They taste of meat, yet of flour. They are wet, yet they are dry. They have weight, but they are light. Airy, yet substantial. Earth, air, fire, water; velvet and elastic! Meat, wheat and magic! They are our family glory!

—Robert P. Tristram Coffin

From a sign at Bagel Connection in New Haven, CT:
Protect your bagels, put lox on them.

—anonymous

The bagel [is] an unsweetened doughnut with rigor mortis.

—Beatrice and Henry Ira Freeman

We have cowboys coming in who have heard about bagels through word of mouth. They'll ask for a "bangle" or a "bockle," but after their first bite they love it. They come back.

—Hershel Shapiro

No man is lonely while eating spaghetti.

—Robert Morley

Everything you see I owe to spaghetti.

—Sophia Loren

Love is grand, but love with lukshen is even better. (Lukshen are a type of noodle.)

—Yiddish Proverb

Simmer til you can't stand it any more, then take it off the fire and dive in.
—Ernest Matthew Mickler

On the food at his restaurant, Trader Vic's:
The real, native South Seas food is lousy. You can't eat it.
—Victor J. (Trader Vic) Bergeron

If it weren't for Philo T. Farnsworth, inventor of television, we'd still be eating frozen radio dinners.
—Johnny Carson

I personally prefer a nice frozen TV Dinner at home, mainly because it's so little trouble. All you have to do is have another drink while you're throwing it in the garbage.
—Jack Douglas

Next to getting warm and keeping warm, dinner and supper were the most interesting things we had to think about. Our lives centered around warmth and food and the return of the men at nightfall.
—Willa Cather

There is nothing better on a cold wintry day than a properly made pot pie.
—Craig Claiborne

Man is the only animal that can remain on friendly terms with the victims he intends to eat until he eats them.

—Samuel Butler

And that reminds me of that wonderful little lamb stew I had the other night at Chuck Williams'—it was so wonderful you could cuddle it in your arms.

—James Beard

God sends meat and the devil sends cooks.
—Thomas Deloney

If you throw a lamb chop in the oven, what's to keep it from getting done?

—Joan Crawford

Poor men want meat for their stomachs, rich men stomachs for their meat.

—Anthony Copley

The nearer the bone the sweeter the meat.

—English Proverb

You must reflect carefully beforehand with whom you are to eat and drink, rather than what you are to eat and drink. For a dinner of meats without the company of a friend is like the life of a lion or a wolf.

—Epicurus

Roast Beef, Medium, is not only a food. It is a philosophy. Seated at Life's Dining Table, with the menu of Morals before you, your eye wanders a bit over the *entrées*, the *hors d'oeuvres*, and the things *à la* though you know the Roast Beef, Medium, is safe and sane, and sure.

—Edna Ferber

Beef is the soul of cooking.

—Marie Antoine Carême

Talk of joy: there may be things better than beef stew and baked potatoes and home-made bread—there may be.

—David Grayson

Old friendships are like meats served up repeatedly, cold, comfortless, and distasteful. The stomach turns against them.

—William Hazlitt

The feeling of friendship is like that of being comfortably filled with roast beef; love, like being enlivened with champagne.

—Samuel Johnson

I had read somewhere that President Eisenhower's technique for broiling steaks was to pitch them directly into a blazing fire and dust them off with a whisk broom when they were done to his taste. I followed the presidential recipe with disastrous results. Ike, I concluded, either didn't know beans about beef or didn't use busted-up fruit crates and his landlady's bordello-baroque furniture for firewood.

—Jay Jacobs

Any of us would kill a cow rather than not have beef.

—Samuel Johnson

What say you to a piece of beef and mustard?

—William Shakespeare

Mustard's no good without roast beef.

—Chico Marx

What avails it us to have our bellies full of meat if it be not digested?

—Michel de Montaigne

'Tis not the meat, but 'tis the appetite
Makes eating a delight.

—Sir John Suckling

God sendeth and giveth both mouth and meat.

—Thomas Tusser

On fads in cooking:
A few years ago it was considered chic to serve Beef Wellington; fortunately, like Napoleon, it met its Waterloo.

—René Veaux

RECIPE FOR *BOILED BOAR**

Ingredients:
8 gallons sea water
2 pounds rock salt
1 hard-boiled hen's egg
2 gallons red wine
1 boar*
3 sprigs laurel mustard
   vinegar

After boar is prepared for cooking, prepare the sea water. Pound up the rock salt in a mortar, then mix with the sea water and stir with a stick until the boiled hen's egg will float on it. Add the wine to the mixture, then heat in a large vessel until boiling. Boil the boar in the liquid, adding the sprigs of laurel. When tender, remove from pan and skin the boar. Serve on a central platter with salt, mustard, and vinegar, with boiled boar sauce.

[*Not to be confused with a wild bore although, under the proper circumstances, either may do.]

—Apicius (Marcus Gavius Apicius) *The Roman Cookery Book* circa A.D. 14

Even as the eye glistened and the mouth began to water at the sight of a noble roast of beef, all crisp and crackly in its cold succulence, the attention was diverted to a plump broiled chicken, whose brown and crackly tenderness fairly seemed to beg for the sweet and savory pillage of the tooth. But now a pungent and exciting fragrance would assail the nostrils: it was the smoked pink slices of an Austrian ham—should it be the brawny beef, now, or the juicy breast of a white tender pullet, or should it be the smoky pungency, the half nostalgic savor of the Austrian ham?

—Thomas Wolfe

Veal is the quintessential Lonely Guy meat. There's something pale and lonely about it, especially if it doesn't have any veins. It's so wan and Kierkegaardian. You just know it's not going to hurt you.

—Bruce Jay Friedman

Passionate claims by various regional chauvinists notwithstanding, the pig, not the steer or any other quadruped, is the supreme vehicle for the barbecue....For optimal enjoyment, barbecue also should be unmanageably sloppy, as it is at its best in the Carolinas.

—Jay Jacobs

He who cannot eat horsemeat need not do so. Let him eat pork. But he who cannot eat pork, let him eat horsemeat. It's simply a question of taste.

—Nikita S. Khrushchev

I believe that eating pork makes people stupid.

—David Steinberg

Who will join me in a dish of tripe? It soothes, appeases the anger of the outraged, stills the fear of death, and reminds us of tripe eaten in former days, when there was always a half-filled pot of it on the stove.

—Günter Grass

Leopold Bloom ate with relish the inner organs of beasts and fowls. He liked thick giblet soup, nutty gizzards, a stuffed roast heart, liver slices fried with breadcrumbs, fried hencod's roe. Most of all he liked grilled mutton kidneys which gave to his palate a fine tang of scented urine.

—James Joyce

> Catius is ever moral, ever grave,
> Thinks who endures a knave, is next a knave,
> Save just at dinner—then prefers, no doubt,
> A rogue with venison to a saint without.

—Alexander Pope

THE ENTIRE RECIPE FOR *BOILED OWL*

Take feathers off. Clean owl and put in cooking pot with lots of water. Add salt to taste.

—*The Eskimo Cookbook* (1952)

Quoted from his address to Le Club des Chefs des Chefs:
We had too much camel in the fridge, so I tried some ways to preserve it.
—Otto Goebel

I don't go for the nouvelle approach—serving a rabbit rump with coffee extract sauce and a slice of kiwi fruit.
—Jeff Smith (The Frugal Gourmet)

When I demanded of my friend what viands he preferred,
He quoth: "A large cold bottle, and a small hot bird!"
—Eugene Field

You first parents of the human race...who ruined yourself for an apple, what might you not have done for a truffled turkey?
—Brillat-Savarin

It was dramatic to watch [grandmother] decapitate [a turkey] with an axe on the day before Thanksgiving. Nowadays the expense of hiring grandmothers for the ax work would probably qualify all turkeys so honored with "gourmet" status.
—Russell Baker

On the best way to thaw a frozen turkey:
Blow in its ear.
—Johnny Carson

A goose is a silly bird, too much for one, not enough for two.

—Anthony Poole

RECIPE FOR *BOILED PARROT*

Pluck the parrot, then wash and truss the drawn bird. Place in a pan and well cover with water, to which may be added vinegar and a little dill.

When partly cooked, make a bouquet of leek and coriander and boil with the bird.

While the parrot is cooking, put pepper, caraway seed, coriander, rue, asafoetida, and mint in a mortar and pound to a paste. Moisten with vinegar, add dates well-shredded.

Remove parrot from pan, and use water remaining to thin the sauce. Thicken with corn flour.

Pour thickened sauce over the bird and serve immediately. The same recipe can be used for flamingo.

—Apicius (Marcus Gavius Apicius) *The Roman Cookery Book* circa A.D. 14

It is to be regretted that domestication has seriously deteriorated the moral character of the duck. In a wild state, he is a faithful husband...but no sooner is he domesticated than he becomes polygamous, and makes nothing of owning ten or a dozen wives at a time.

—Mrs. Isabella Beeton

Six white pigeons to be smothered, to be plucked, to be cleaned and all this to be accomplished before Gertrude Stein returned for she didn't like to see work being done.

—Alice B. Toklas

We didn't starve, but we didn't eat chicken unless we were sick, or the chicken was.

—Bernard Malamud

Only a Southerner knows how to fry chicken. Period!

—anonymous

And we meet, with champagne and a chicken, at last.

—Mary Wortley Montagu

I want there to be no peasant in my kingdom so poor that he is unable to have a chicken in his pot on Sundays.

—King Henry IV of France

Presidential campaign slogan:
A chicken in every pot.

—Herbert Hoover

Gorbachev has a new slogan: A chicken in every time zone.

—Johnny Carson

The fricassee with dumplings is made by a Mrs. Miller whose husband has left her four times on account of her disposition and returned four times on account of her cooking and is still there.

—Rex Stout

The carp was dead, killed, assassinated, murdered in the first, second and third degree. Limp, I fell into a chair, with my hands still unwashed reached for a cigarette, lighted it, and waited for the police to come and take me into custody.

—Alice B. Toklas

They fried the fish with bacon and were astonished; for no fish had ever seemed so delicious before. They did not know that the quicker a fresh water fish is on the fire after he is caught the better he is; and they reflected little upon what a sauce open air sleeping, open air exercise, bathing, and a large ingredient of hunger makes, too.

—Mark Twain

Suggesting how to best cook soft-shell crabs:
The best thing is not to do anything interesting.

—Terrence Conway

Referring to George Morfogen, his assistant manager at the Terminal Oyster Bar in Grand Central Station, New York. His responsibilities include the weekly purchase of $24,000 of fresh seafood:
George knows everything about every fish that comes in here—where they came from, what they were doing before they were caught, who their mothers and fathers were.

—Stanley Kramer

If it swims, it's edible.

—Bill Demmond

Fish should smell like the tide. Once they smell like fish, it's too late.

—Oscar Gizelt

In Mexico we have a word for sushi: bait.

—José Simon

In Japan, chefs offer the flesh of the puffer fish, or *fugu*, which is highly poisonous unless prepared with exquisite care. The most distinguished chefs leave just enough of the poison in the flesh to make the diner's lips tingle, so that they know how close they are coming to their mortality. Sometimes, of course, a diner comes too close, and each year a certain number of *fugu*-lovers die in midmeal.

—Diane Ackerman

To the goggling unbeliever [Texans] say—as people always say about their mangier dishes—"but it's just like chicken, only tenderer." Rattlesnake is, in fact, just like chicken, only tougher.

—Alistair Cooke

FUGU! A TASTE TO DIE FOR...

Passions and pleasures of the cultured palate often go unappreciated by the large gray masses of humanity. Tastes that entice some repulse others because of differences in lifestyles and mores, breeding and fashion. Few food fads, however, have the grave or immediate consequences of belonging to the Japanese cult of *fugukien* who worship and lionize the little puffer fish or fugu, among other ways, by eating it raw.

So what's wrong with a little sushi? Ordinarily nothing, except that the ugly little puffer fish, when improperly prepared, is very poisonous. In fact, the fugu is the most poisonous sea creature in existence, with a toxin 275 times more lethal than cyanide. There is no antidote for the death by paralysis which can take a few brief minutes or leave the diner, who is fully aware of what is happening, lingering on for as long as six torturous hours.

In Japan, where the fish is a delicacy, diners pay $150 per person and up for a complete fugu meal. Chefs are legally forbidden to prepare and serve fugu, but are convinced and coerced by various means to do so, to the tune of $50 million annually—the estimated yearly take for the fugu industry in Japan.

There is greater relish for the earliest fruit of the season.

—Martial

O Autumn, laden with fruit, and stained
With the blood of the grape, pass not, but sit
Beneath my shady roof; there thou may'st rest
And tune thy jolly voice to my fresh pipe,
And all the daughters of the year shall dance!
Sing now the lusty song of fruits and flowers.

—William Blake

Ignorance is like the delicate exotic fruit; touch it and the bloom is gone.

—Oscar Wilde

When one has tasted watermelons, one knows what angels eat. It was not a Southern watermelon that Eve took; we know it because she repented.

—Mark Twain

In watermelon sugar the deeds were done and done again as my life is done in watermelon sugar.

—Richard Brautigan

O precious food! Delight of the mouth!
Oh, much better than gold, masterpiece of Apollo!
O flower of all the fruits! O ravishing melon!

—Marc Antoine de Saint-Amant

When walking through a melon patch, don't adjust your sandals.
—Chinese Proverb

Friends are like melons. Shall I tell you why?
To find one good you must a hundred try.
—Claude Mermet

**He who fills his stomach with melons is like
him who fills it with light—there is a blessing in it.
—Arab Proverb**

Success to me is having ten honeydew melons and eating only the top half
of each one.

—Barbra Streisand

Raspberries are best not washed. After all, one must have faith in something.

—Ann Batchelder

Nobody can be insulted by raspberries and cream.

—Barbara Kafka

Strawberries, and only strawberries, could now be thought or spoken of. "The best fruit in England—everybody's favourite—always wholesome. These the finest beds and finest sorts. Delightful to gather oneself—the only way of really enjoying them. Morning decidedly the best time—never tired—every sort good—hautboy infinitely superior—no comparison—the others hardly eatable—hautboys very scarce—Chili preferred—white wood finest flavour of all—price of strawberries in London...only objection to gathering strawberries the stooping—glaring sun—tired to death—could bear it no longer—must go and sit in the shade." Such, for half an hour, was the conversation.

—Jane Austen

The Strawberry is not everyone's fruit. To some it brings a sudden rash, and to others twinges of rheumatism. This fact must be admitted and faced.

—Edward Bunyard

On strawberries:
Doubtless God could have made a better berry, but doubtless God never did.

—William Butler

Toujours strawberries and cream.

—Samuel Johnson

Adam was but human—this explains it all. He did not want the apple for the apple's sake, he wanted it only because it was forbidden.

—Mark Twain

All the evil in the world was brought in by means of an apple.

—Medieval Proverb

> Of man's first disobedience, and the fruit
> Of that forbidden tree, whose mortal taste
> Brought death into the world, and all our woe...
>
> —Milton

Comfort me with apples: for I am sick of love.
—The Song of Solomon

It is more pleasant to pluck an apple from the branch than to take one from a graven dish.

—Ovid

I love fruit, when it's expensive.

—Sir Arthur Wing Pinero

I will make an end of my dinner; there's pippins and cheese to come.

—William Shakespeare

> With heart that is true,
> I'll be waiting for you,
> In the shade of the old apple tree.
> —Harry Williams

What is more mortifying than to feel that you've missed the plum for want of courage to shake the tree?

—Logan Pearsall Smith

My father cut down a magnificent plum tree which every year had given us a bountiful harvest of sweet juicy blue or red plums, I have forgotten which, and every second or third year, I have forgotten which again, a bumper crop, in order to make room for a backyard garage. The car it contained was only a Maxwell. A whole fleet of Rolls Royces would not have compensated for the home-made fresh plum ice cream which disappeared with our tree.

—Waverley Root

The pear is the grandfather of the apple, its poor relation, a fallen aristocrat, the man-at-arms of our domains, which once, in our humid land, lived lonely and lordly, preserving the memory of it's prestige by its haughty comportment.

—François Pierre de La Varenne

An apple is an excellent thing—until you have tried a peach!

—George du Maurier

Peel a fig for your friend, a peach for your enemy.

—John Ray

I remember his showing me how to eat a peach by building a little white mountain of sugar and then dipping the peach into it.

—Mary McCarthy

Talking of Pleasure, this moment I was writing with one hand, and with the other holding to my Mouth a Nectarine—how good, how fine. It went down all pulpy, slushy, oozy—all its delicious embonpoint melted down my throat like a large, beatified Strawberry.

—John Keats

You have to ask children and birds how cherries and strawberries taste.

—Goethe

A Peach of a President

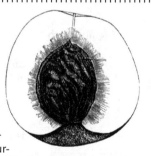

Thomas Jefferson, although sometimes reputed to have been the White House's greatest epicure, actually was a man of simple tastes. Central to his diet was the notion that, above all, food, and especially produce, had to be fresh. So much did he rely on produce that many White House menus during his term in office were almost completely vegetarian. His particular penchant was for fresh fruit, and he was responsible for importing several varieties to America including peaches. His Monticello estate alone came to boast 1100 peach trees during his lifetime.

I came across excellent blackberries,—ate of them heartily. It was midday, & when I left the brambles, I found I had a sufficient meal so there was no need to go to an inn. Of a sudden it struck me as an extraordinary thing. Here I had satisfied my hunger without payment, without indebtedness to any man. The vividness with which I felt that this was extraordinary seems to me a shrewd comment on a social state which practically denies a man's right to food unless he have money.

—George Gissing

What is more melancholy than the old apple trees that linger about the spot where once stood a homestead, but where there is now a ruined chimney rising out of a grassy and weed-grown cellar? They offer their fruit to every wayfarer—apples that are bittersweet with the moral of time's vicissitude.

—Nathaniel Hawthorne

> The apples that grew on the fruit-tree of knowledge
> By woman were pluck'd, and she still wears the prize
> To tempt us in theatre, senate, or college—
> I mean the love-apples that bloom in the eyes.
> —Horace and James Smith

The apples on the other side of the wall are always the sweetest.

—W.G. Benham

> Blossom of the almond trees,
> April's gift to April's bees.
> —Edwin Arnold

Durian and Brazil Nut. An odd pair? Yes, but they have this in common, that you have to be careful they don't drop on your head.

—Alan Davidson

An apple-pie without some cheese
Is like a kiss without a squeeze.

—anonymous

But I, when I undress me
Each night, upon my knees
Will ask the Lord to bless me
With apple pie and cheese!

—Eugene Field

Goat cheese...produced a bizarre eating era when sensible people insisted that this miserable cheese produced by these miserable creatures reared on miserable hardscrabble earth was actually superior to the magnificent creamy cheeses of the noblest dairy animals bred in the richest green valleys of the earth.

—Russell Baker

Cheese is probably the friendliest of foods. It endears itself to everything and never tires of showing off to great advantage. Any liquor or, I may say, any potable or any edible loves to be seen in the company of cheese. Naturally, some nationalities choose one type of companion and some another, but you very seldom find clashes of temperament in passing.

—James Beard

The great Norman cheeses were served as well: Camembert, Pont l'Évêque, and the stinky Livarot. But my father warned: "Not for Mademoiselle Simone, the strong cheeses." He thought young girls shouldn't be allowed to pollute their mouths with smelly odors.

—Simone Beck

Poets have been mysteriously silent on the subject of cheese.

—G.K. Chesterton

> *Many's the long night I've dreamed of cheese—*
> *toasted, mostly.*
> *—Robert Louis Stevenson*

On how to test the ripeness of Camembert cheese:
You put your left index finger on your eye and your right index finger on the cheese...if they sort of feel the same, the cheese is ready.

—M. Taittinger

People who know nothing about cheeses reel away from Camembert, Roquefort and Stilton because the plebeian proboscis is not equipped to differentiate between the sordid and the sublime.

—Harvey Day

How can one conceive of a one-party system in a country that has over 200 varieties of cheese?

—Charles de Gaulle

162

Brie with the rind sliced off is among the most essential tokens of yuppiedom.

—Stratford P. Sherman

Some people want to see God with their eyes as they see a cow, and love Him as they love a cow—for the milk and cheese and profit it brings them.

—Meister Eckhart

A cheese may disappoint. It may be dull, it may be naïve, it may be oversophisticated. Yet it remains cheese—milk's leap toward immortality.

—Clifton Fadiman

Never commit yourself to a cheese without having first *examined* it.

—T.S. Eliot

The obscure man's reflections may be as wise as the rich cheese-maker's, on everything but cheese.

—Henry S. Haskins

Processed "cheese." The word should always, like Soviet "democracy," be framed in quotes, for no matter what the law may say, I refuse to call this cheese....The best I can say for it is that it is not poisonous; the worst, that it represents the triumph of technology over conscience.

In the preparation of this solidified floor wax...every problem but one is solved: packaging, keeping, distribution, slicing, cost. One problem alone is not solved: that of making cheese.

—Bob Brown

What Freud was to psychoanalysis, I was to wine.

—Sam Aaron

Without bread, without wine, love is nothing.
—French Proverb

The wines that one remembers best are not necessarily the finest that one has tasted, and the highest quality may fail to delight so much as some far more humble beverage drunk in more favourable company.

—H. Warner Allen

Religions change; beer and wine remain.

—Hervey Allen

The vine bears three kinds of grapes: the first of pleasure, the second of intoxication, the third of disgust.

—Anacharsis

Wine is man's most successful effort to translate the perishable into the permanent.

—John Arlott

On why he sells wine at farmers' markets:
Bread and wine and thou—it's all there.

—Barry Benepe

The soft extractive note of an aged cork being withdrawn has the true sound of a man opening his heart.

—William Samuel Benwell

Every man at the beginning doth set forth good wine; and when men have well drunk, then that which is worse: but thou hast kept the good wine until now.

—The Bible

Burgundy makes you think of silly things; Bordeaux makes you talk about them; and Champagne makes you do them.

—Brillat-Savarin

To buy very good wine nowadays requires only money. To serve it to your guests is a sign of fatigue.

—William F. Buckley, Jr.

Excellent wine generates enthusiasm. And whatever you do with enthusiasm is generally successful.

—Philippe de Rothschild

On the movement to substitute bottle caps for corks:
Can you imagine opening a bottle of champagne with a bottle opener? I can't. It would eliminate half the fun.

—Alain de Vogue

I like best the wine drunk at the cost of others.

—Diogenes, The Cynic (Diogenes Laertius)

"I rather like bad wine," said Mr. Mountchesney; "one gets so bored with good wine."

—Benjamin Disraeli

Wine is a precarious aphrodisiac, and its fumes have blighted many a mating.

—Norman Douglas

In Bordeaux, as in the rest of France, the marriage of food and wine is celebrating hundreds of years of happiness. If there is relatively little thrill or experimentation, well, that's the way it often is with successful long-term marriages. But there's plenty of ease, comfort and pleasure of partners content with each other.

—Florence Fabricant

A bottle of wine begs to be shared: I have never met a miserly wine lover.

—Clifton Fadiman

On wine:
Poetry in a bottle.

—Clifton Fadiman

> *Wine is sunlight, held together by water.*
> *—Galileo*

To take wine into our mouths is to savor a droplet of the river of human history.

—Clifton Fadiman

Wine makes daily living easier, less hurried, with fewer tensions and more tolerance.

—Benjamin Franklin

Fine wine must be treated like a lovely woman in bed.

—French Proverb

From wine what sudden friendship springs!

—John Gay

I am beauty and love;
I am friendship, the comforter;
I am that which forgives and forgets.
The Spirit of Wine.

—W.E. Henley

The essence of pleasure does not lie in the thing enjoyed, but in the accompanying consciousness. If I had a humble spirit in my service, who, when I asked for a glass of water, brought me the world's costliest wines blended in a chalice, I should dismiss him, in order to teach him that pleasure consists not in what I enjoy, but in having my own way.

—Sören Kierkegaard

One barrel of wine can work more miracles than a church full of saints.

—Italian Proverb

Wine is the pleasantest subject in the world to discuss. All its associations are with occasions when people are at their best; with relaxation, contentment, leisurely meals and the free flow of ideas.

—Hugh Johnson

Wine gives a man nothing. It neither gives him knowledge nor wit; it only animates a man, and enables him to bring out what a dread of the company has repressed. This is one of the disadvantages of wine: it makes a man mistake words for thoughts.

—Samuel Johnson

Diogenes was asked what wine he liked best; and he answered as I would have done when he said: "Somebody else's."

—Michel de Montaigne

Bordeaux calls to mind a distinguished figure in a frock coat....He enters his moderate enthusiasms in a leather pocketbook, observing the progress of beauty across his palate like moves in a game of chess.

—Frank J. Prial

Like footmen and upstairs maids, wine stewards are portrayed as acolytes of the privileged, ever eager to intimidate and spurn the unwary.

—Frank J. Prial

The more specific the name, the better the wine.

—Frank Schoonmaker

A glass of good wine is a gracious creature, and reconciles poor mortality to itself, and that is what few things can do.

—Sir Walter Scott

Happiness is a wine of the rarest vintage, and seems insipid to a vulgar taste.

—Logan Pearsall Smith

What is the definition of a good wine? It should start and end with a smile.

—William Sokolin

The advantage of champagne consists not only in the exhilarating sparkle and play of its mantling life, where the beads that airily rise ever in pursuit of those that have merrily passed; but in the magnetism it possesses above all other wines—of tempting the fair sex to drink an extra glass.

—Saint Ange

And every day when I've been good,
I get an orange after food.
—Robert Louis Stevenson

Wine is bottled poetry.

—Robert Louis Stevenson

This wine should be eaten, it is too good to be drunk.

—Jonathan Swift

Chardonnay is a red wine masquerading as a white, and Pinot Noir is a white wine masquerading as a red.

—André Tchelistcheff

You'll have no scandal while you dine,
But honest talk and wholesome wine.
—Alfred Lord Tennyson

I like to shock people—especially with dessert. To start with a simple theme and then do something shocking. If you really know the classics, then you can vary as you like.

—Charles Palmer

On his mother's skill with dessert:
She could make jello, for instance, with sliced peaches hanging in it, peaches just suspended there, in defiance of the law of gravity. She could bake a cake that tasted like a banana.

—Philip Roth

It sits as lightly on a heavy meal as it does on you conscience.
—Advertisement for Jell-O™ brand gelatin

The most dangerous food is wedding cake.

—American Proverb

RECIPE FOR *CLOUTED CREAME*

Take your milke being new milked; and presentlie set it upon the fire from morning until the evening. But let it not seeth: and this is called my Ladie Young's clouted creame.
—Sir Hugh Platt, *Delightes for Ladies, to Adorne Their Persons, Tables, Closets, and Distillatories, With, Bewties, Banquets, Perfumes, and Waters* (1600)

A great empire, like a great cake, is most easily diminished at the edges.
—Benjamin Franklin

It's paradoxical, but diminished expectations seem to make for more happiness. You don't expect to eat birthday cake every night. And, actually, in the periods of your life when you did eat birthday cake every night, you were sick. It's not actually very rewarding to eat birthday cake like that.
—Michael Crichton

All millionaires love a baked apple.
—Ronald Firbank

The friendly cow all red and white,
I love with all my heart:
She gives me cream with all her might
To eat with apple-tart.
—Robert Louis Stevenson

The difference between Los Angeles and yogurt is that yogurt has an active, living culture.

—anonymous

What is a roofless cathedral compared to a well-built pie?
—William Maginn

Of late the cook has had the surprising sagacity to learn from the French that apples will make pyes; and it's a question, if, in the violence of his efforts, we do not get one of apples, instead of having both of beef-steak which I prefer.

—George Washington

I prefer Hostess™ fruit pies to pop-up toaster tarts because they don't require so much cooking.

—Carrie Snow

American Danish can be doughy, heavy, sticky, tasting of prunes and is usually wrapped in cellophane. Danish Danish is light, crisp, buttery and often tastes of marzipan or raisins; it is seldom wrapped in anything but loving care.

—R.W. Apple, Jr.

Older women are like aging strudels—the crust may not be so lovely, but the filling has come at last into its own.

—Robert Farrar Capon

For months they have lain in wait, dim shapes lurking in the forgotten corners of houses and factories all over the country and now they are upon us, sodden with alcohol, their massive bodies bulging with strange green protuberances, attacking us in our homes, at our friends' homes, at our offices—there is no escape, it is the hour of the fruitcake.

—Deborah Papier

While an eon, as someone has observed, may be two people and a ham, a fruitcake is forever.

—Russell Baker

A cook can make a difference. A custard is more than the sum of its yolk and sugar parts.

—Raymond Sokolov

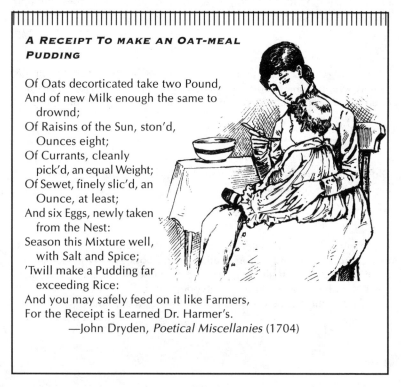

A RECEIPT TO MAKE AN OAT-MEAL PUDDING

Of Oats decorticated take two Pound,
And of new Milk enough the same to
   drownd;
Of Raisins of the Sun, ston'd,
   Ounces eight;
Of Currants, cleanly
   pick'd, an equal Weight;
Of Sewet, finely slic'd, an
   Ounce, at least;
And six Eggs, newly taken
   from the Nest:
Season this Mixture well,
   with Salt and Spice;
'Twill make a Pudding far
   exceeding Rice:
And you may safely feed on it like Farmers,
For the Receipt is Learned Dr. Harmer's.
     —John Dryden, *Poetical Miscellanies* (1704)

Custard: A detestable substance produced by a malevolent conspiracy of the hen, the cow, and the cook.

—Ambrose Bierce

Never tell, but I'll make her a pudding, a pudding she'll like, too, and I'll pay for it myself; so mind you see she eats it. Many a one has been comforted in their sorrow by seeing a good dish come upon the table.

—E.S. Gaskell

In moments of considerable strain I tend to take bread-and-butter pudding. There is something about the blandness of soggy bread, the crispness of the golden outer crust and the unadulterated pleasure of lightly set custard that makes the world seem a better place to live.

—Clement Freud

While Honey lies in Every Flower, no doubt,
It takes a Bee to get the Honey out.
—Arthur Gutterman

The bee that hath honey in her mouth, hath a sting in her tail.

—John Lyly

Plain food is quite enough for me;
    Three courses are as good as ten:—
If Nature can subsist on three,
    Thank Heaven for three. Amen!
I always thought cold victual nice;—
My choice would be vanilla-ice.
—Oliver Wendell Holmes, Sr.

WE ALL SCREAM FOR...

Dolley Madison's name may be the one most associated with it, but even President George Washington loved ice cream. According to one account he spent $200 on it in one summer alone...and that was when $200 was $200!

The first known directions written in an English cookbook for making ice cream go as follows:

Pare, stone, and scald twelve ripe Apricots, beat them fine in a Marble Mortar, put to them six Ounces of double refined Sugar, a Pint of scalding Cream. Work it through a Hair Sieve, then put it into a Tin which has a close Cover, set it in a Tube of Ice broken small, and a large quantity of Salt put amongst it. When you see your Cream grow thick around the Edges of your Tin, stir it, and set it in again 'till it all grows quite thick.

When your Cream is all Froze up, take it out of your Tin, and put it in the Mould you intend it to be turned out of. Then put on the Lid, and have ready another Tub with Ice and Salt in as before. Put your Mould in the Middle, and lay your Ice under and over it. Let it stand for five Hours. Dip your Tin in warm Water when you turn it out. If it be Summer, you must not turn it out 'till the Moment you want it.

You may use any Sort of Fruit if you have not Apricots, only observe to work it fine.

—Elizabeth Raffald, *The Experienced English House-Keeper, for the Use and Ease of Ladies, House-Keepers, Cooks, &c. Wrote Purely from Practice* (1769)

Referring to her penchant for sweets:
I derived my pleasure from my indulgence.

—Dolley Madison

Then, as though touching her waist had reminded her of something, she felt in the pocket of her overalls and produced a small slab of chocolate. She broke it in half and gave one of the pieces to Winston. Even before he had taken it he knew by the smell that it was a very unusual chocolate. It was dark and shiny and wrapped in silver paper. Chocolate normally was dull-brown crumbly stuff that tasted, as nearly as one could describe it, like the smoke of a rubbish fire. But at some time or another he had tasted chocolate like the piece she had given him. The first whiff of its scent had stirred up some memory which he could not pin down, but which was powerful and troubling.

—George Orwell

Coffee: Induces wit. Good only if it comes through Havre. After a big dinner party it is taken standing up. Take it without sugar—very swank: gives the impression you have lived in the East.

—Gustave Flaubert

Only Irish coffee provides in a single glass all four essential food groups: alcohol, caffeine, sugar, and fat.

—Alex Levine

Good coffee is like friendship: rich and warm and strong.
—Advertisement for the Pan-American Coffee Bureau

THE WINE OF ARABY

Legend has it that the first of God's creatures to know the pleasures of "qahway" (or as we know it, coffee) was the goat. A young Arab goatherder, Kaldi, after tending his herd for some time, took note of the strange dancing behavior his goats exhibited after eating the crimson berries from a bush he had never seen before. Eating some of the berries himself, Kaldi soon joined them, dancing as it were, under the hot desert sun.

Stumbling upon this merriment one day, a Moslem mullah inquired if Kaldi and his flock had, to put it politely, been out in the sun too long. Kaldi told the holy man of the red berries and the two parted company.

The daily practice of Islam is built around a cycle of prayer. Depending upon the particular sect of Islam, the amount of time spent each day on prayer and meditation can be long and arduous. As it was, later that same day, the holy man in our story fell asleep in the mosque during prayers. Allah, it seemed, had been noticing this growing tendency among his faithful of late and was not especially pleased by it. So during his mullah's nap, he sent the prophet Mohammed to the holy man in his dreams to deliver a message. The prophet explained Allah's position on sleep and prayer and suggested that the mullah gather some of Kaldi's berries, boil them in water, drink the potion, and then pray. With the recipe came a guarantee that the mullah and his congregation would be wide awake from that day forward. And so it was.

Islam's prohibition against the ingestion of wine or alcohol saw the new beverage make its way out of the mosque and into Arab homes in short order. With its popularity came the name for the new potion—the "wine of Araby" or, to be somewhat more linguistically precise, the "qahway of Araby".

By the time Columbus and his followers began to sail the ocean blue, the seeds and green beans of the qahway plant were also being used by the faithful to make their holy beverage. As the wheels of commerce grinded forward, the drink's popularity spread by merchants in the 1600s to Europe where qahway was phoneticized, with its typical Western accuracy, into the word coffee.

Back in the Arab world though, the little bean's fame created a new problem—the "faithful" were spending less time in the mosque and too much time in the newfound network of coffeehouses, complete with an assortment of dancers, singers, and gamblers—none of which pleased the Islamic leaders of the 17th century. As is the case with so many good things, the holy men tried to outlaw coffee. Fortunately, the Caliph of Cairo, the dominant leader of most of the Muslim world at that time and a direct descendant of Mohammed himself, was also an ardent coffee addict and so quashed the brewing holy war that no doubt would have followed this futile act of prohibition.

Coffee should be black as Hell, strong as death, and sweet as love.
—Turkish Proverb

A cup of coffee—real coffee—home-browned, home-ground, home made, that comes to you dark as a hazel-eye, but changes to a golden bronze as you temper it with cream that never cheated, but was real cream from its birth, thick, tenderly yellow, perfectly sweet, neither lumpy nor frothing on the Java: such a cup of coffee is a match for twenty blue devils and will exorcise them all.

—Henry Ward Beecher

A cup of coffee detracts nothing from your intellect; on the contrary your stomach is freed by it and no longer distresses your brain; it will not hamper your mind with troubles but give freedom to its working. Suave molecules of Mocha stir up your blood without causing excessive heat; the organ of thought receives from it a feeling of sympathy; work becomes easier and you will sit down without distress to your principal repast which will restore your body and afford you a calm delicious night.

—Talleyrand

Among the numerous luxuries of the table, unknown to our forefathers, coffee may be considered as one of the most valuable. Its taste is very agreeable, and its flavour uncommonly so; but its principle excellence depends on its salubrity, and on its exhilarating quality. It excites cheerfulness, without intoxication; and the pleasing flow of spirits which it occasions...is never followed by sadness, languor or debility. It diffuses over the whole frame a glow of health, and sense of ease and well-being which is extremely delightful: existence is felt to be a positive enjoyment, and the mental powers are awakened and rendered uncommonly active.

—Benjamin Thompson

Last words:
I feel the end approaching. Quick, bring me my dessert, coffee, and liqueur.

—Pierette Brillat-Savarin

On a sheep-cropped knoll under a clump of elms we ate the strawberries and drank the wine—as Sebastian promised, they were delicious together—and we lit fat, Turkish cigarettes and lay on our backs, Sebastian's eyes on the leaves above him, mine on his profile, while the blue-grey smoke rose, untroubled by any wind, to the blue-green shadows of foliage, and the sweet scent of the tobacco merged with the sweet summer scents around us and the fumes of the sweet, golden wine seemed to lift us a finger's breadth above the turf and hold us suspended.

—Evelyn Waugh

Drink helps us to penetrate the veil; it gives us glimpses of the Magi of creation where they sit weaving their spells and sowing their seeds of incantation to the flowing mind.

—Don Marquis

Goes down better than the real thing.®
—Advertisement for Titanic Beer.™

If you find an Australian indoors, it's a fair bet that he will have a glass in his hand.

—Jonathan Aitken

I'll eat when I'm hungry and drink when I'm dry,
If moonshine don't kill me, I'll live till I die.
—American Folk Song, anonymous

Eating and drinking hold body and soul together.
—Alsatian Proverb (Alsace-Lorraine)

Drinking when we are not thirsty and making love at all seasons, madam: that is all there is to distinguish us from other animals.
—Pierre de Beaumarchais

The human intellect owes its superiority over that of the lower animals in great measure to the stimulus which alcohol has given to imagination— imagination being little else than another name for illusion.
—Samuel Butler

Gin-and-water is the source of all my inspiration.
—Lord Byron

Drinking is in reality an occupation which employs a considerable portion of the time of many people; and to conduct it in the most rational and agreeable manner is one of the great arts of living.
—James Boswell

Often Daddy sat up very late working on a case of Scotch.
—Robert Benchley

Upon being warned that drink was "slow poison":
So who's in a hurry?
—Robert Benchley

RECIPE FOR *METHEGLIN**

In sixty gallons of water, boil ten handfuls of sweet briar leaves, Eye-bright, Liverwort, Agrimony, Scabious, Balm, Betony, Strawberry-leaves, Burnet, each four handfuls. Of Mint, Angelica, Bayes and Wild-thyme, Sweet Marjoram, each two handfuls. Six eringo roots.

When the water has taken the virtue and goodness out of the herbs and roots, let it settle and the next day pour off clear. In every three gallons of it boil one of honey, scumming it well and putting in a little cold water now and again to make the scum rise. Add also some white of eggs.

When it is clear scummed, take it off and let it cool; then work it with Ale yeast.

Turn it up and hang it in a Bag, with Ginger, Cinnamon, Cloves and Cardamon. And as it worketh over, put in some strong Honey-drink warmed. When it works no more stop it up.

[*Based on recipes for a form of Welsh mead, Metheglin was a common staple of English taverns. It had the additional virtue of serving as a medicine, though I'm not sure for what. In either case, hypochondriacs and hedonists alike were apt and able to enjoy it and did.]

—Sir Kenelm Digby, *The Closet of the Eminently Learned Sir Kenelm Digby Kt, Opened: Whereby is Discovered Several Ways of Making Metheglin, Sider, Cherry Wine, etc. Together with Excellent Directions for Cookery— also for Preserving, Conserving, Candying, etc.* (1669)

On attitudes toward drinking in Plains, GA, where according to another citizen, "most everybody who does, pretends they don't":
I know folks all have a tizzy about it, but I like a little bourbon of an evening. It helps me sleep. I don't much care what they say about it.

—Lillian Carter

**I HAVE TAKEN MORE OUT OF ALCOHOL
THAN ALCOHOL HAS TAKEN OUT OF ME.
—WINSTON S. CHURCHILL**

A productive drunk is the bane of moralists.

—anonymous

I have to think hard to name an interesting man who does not drink.

—Richard Burton

Who hath woe? Who hath sorrow? Who hath contentions? Who hath babbling? Who hath wounds without cause? Who hath redness of eyes? They that tarry long at the wine; they that go to seek mixed wine.

—The Bible

Red wine for children, champagne for men, and brandy for soldiers.

—Otto von Bismarck

Written as part of his dissenting opinion in a 6-2 U.S. Supreme Court ruling that limited the power of the states to tax and restrict the liquor business:
I was brought up to believe that Scotch whisky would need a tax preference to survive in competition with Kentucky bourbon.

—Hugo L. Black

Good ale, the true and proper drink of Englishmen. He is not deserving of the name of Englishman who speaketh against ale, that is good ale.

—George Borrow

On raicilla, a 180-proof beverage made from the maguey plant:
If you drink it straight down, you can feel it going into each individual intestine.

—Richard Burton

Like a camel, I can go without a drink for seven days—and have on several horrible occasions.

—Herb Caen

Even for those who dislike Champagne...there are two Champagnes one can't refuse: Dom Perignon and the even superior Cristal, which is bottled in a natural-coloured glass that displays its pale blaze, a chilled fire of such prickly dryness that, swallowed, seems not to have been swallowed at all, but instead to have been turned to vapours on the tongue, and burned there to one sweet ash.

—Truman Capote

In answering a telephone survey:

Do I like champagne? Ah, no, listen, that is a very personal question and one that I am not at liberty to answer....A less intimate question, yes. You should have asked me when I last made love, for example. You should have asked me when I last made love and enjoyed it.

—Henri Cartier-Bresson

I drink when I have occasion, and sometimes when I have no occasion.

—Cervantes

Drink because you are happy, but never because you are miserable.

—G.K. Chesterton

Most people hate the taste of beer—to begin with. It is, however, a prejudice that many people have been able to overcome.

—Winston S. Churchill

Some men are like musical glasses—to produce their finest tones you must keep them wet.

—Samuel Taylor Coleridge

To drink is a Christian diversion, unknown to the Turk or the Persian.

—William Congreve

Whiskey and vermouth cannot meet as friends and the Manhattan is an offense against piety.

—Bernard De Voto

When I die I want to decompose in a barrel of porter and have it served in all the pubs in Dublin. I wonder would they know it was me?

—J.P. Donleavy

Alcohol removes inhibitions—like that scared little mouse who got drunk and shook his whiskers and shouted: "Now bring on the damn cat!"

—Eleanor Early

DON'T DRINK AND...

Don't, when you drink, elevate your glass as if you were going to stand it inverted on your nose. Bring the glass perpendicularly to the lips, and then lift it to a slight angle. Do this easily.

Drink sparingly while eating. It is far better for the digestion not to drink tea or coffee until the meal is finished. Drink gently, and do not pour it down your throat like water turned out of a pitcher.

—Hugo Ziemann, Steward of the White House, and Mrs. F.L. Gillette, *The Original White House Cookbook: Contains Cooking, Toilet and Household Recipes, Menus, Dinner-giving, Table Etiquette, Care of the Sick, Health Suggestions, Facts Worth Knowing, etc.* (1887)

What does drunkenness not accomplish? It unlocks secrets, confirms our hopes, urges the indolent into battle, lifts the burden from anxious minds, teaches new arts.

—Horace

I don't drink; I don't like it—it makes me feel good.

—Oscar Levant

> The man that isn't jolly after drinking
> Is just a drivelling idiot, to my thinking.
> —Euripedes

I have fed purely upon ale; I have eat my ale, drank my ale, and I always sleep upon ale.

—Farquhar

There's no such thing as bad whiskey. Some whiskeys just happen to be better than others. But a man shouldn't fool with booze until he's fifty, and then he's a damn fool if he doesn't.

—William Faulkner

Well, between Scotch and nothin', I suppose I'd take Scotch. It's the nearest thing to good moonshine I can find.

—William Faulkner

Anybody who hates dogs and loves whiskey can't be all bad.

—W.C. Fields

I never drink anything stronger than gin before breakfast.
—W.C. Fields

James Bond:
A martini shaken, not stirred.

—Ian Fleming

On W.C. Field's fondness for aged bourbon:
He has a profound respect for old age. Especially when it's bottled.

—Gene Fowler

I've never been drunk, but often I've been overserved.

—George Gobel

There is nothing for a case of nerves like a case of beer.

—Joan Goldstein

They who drink beer will think beer.

—Washington Irving

Sobriety diminishes, discriminates, and says no; drunkenness expands, unites, and says yes. Not through mere perversity do men run after it.

—William James

Claret is the liquor for boys; port for men; but he who aspires to be a hero must drink brandy.

—Samuel Johnson

As he brews, so shall he drink.

—Ben Jonson

A RECIPE *TO MAKE A SYLLABUB UNDER THE COW*

Put a bottle of strong Beer, and a Pint of Cyder into a Punch Bowl, and grate in a small Nutmeg. Sweeten it to your Taste, then milk as much Milk from the Cow as will make a strong Froth, and the Ale look clear.

Let it stand an Hour, then strew over it a few Currants, well washed, picked, and plumped before the Fire. Then send it to Table.

—Elizabeth Raffald, *The Experienced English House-Keeper, for the Use and Ease of Ladies, House-Keepers, Cooks, &c. Wrote Purely from Practice* (1769)

Even though a number of people have tried, no one has yet found a way to drink for a living.

—Jean Kerr

Drink! for you know not whence you came, nor why; Drink! for you know not why you go, nor where.

—Omar Khayyám

Brandy-and-water spoils two good things.

—Charles Lamb

Whenever someone asks me if I want water with my Scotch, I say I'm thirsty, not dirty.

—Joe E. Lewis

The standard of perfection for vodka (no color, no taste, no smell) was expounded to me long ago by the then Estonian consul-general in New York, and it accounts perfectly for the drink's rising popularity with those who like their alcohol in conjunction with the reassuring tastes of infancy— tomato juice, orange juice, chicken broth. It is the ideal intoxicant for the drinker who wants no reminder of how hurt Mother would be if she knew what he was doing.

—A.J. Liebling

He that eateth well, drinketh well; he that drinketh well, sleepeth well; he that sleepeth well, sinneth not; he that sinneth not goeth straight through Purgatory to Paradise.

—William Lithgow

Life is thirst.

—Leonard Michaels

The great thing about making cognac is that it teaches you above every-thing else to wait—man proposes, but time and God and the seasons have got to be on your side.

—Jean Monnet

Marriage is based on the theory that when a man discovers a brand of beer exactly to his taste he should at once throw up his job and go to work in the brewery.

—George Jean Nathan

There are two reasons for drinking: one is, when you are thirsty, to cure it; the other when you are not thirsty, to prevent it....Prevention is better than cure.

—Thomas Love Peacock

I like to start off my day with a glass of champagne. I like to wind it up with champagne, too. To be frank, I also like a glass or two in between. It may not be the universal medicine for every disease, as my friends the champagne people in Reims and Épernay so often tell me, but it does you less harm than any other liquid.

—Fernand Point

Amusement is the happiness of those that cannot drink.

—Alexander Pope

Appetite comes with eating,...but thirst departs with drinking.

—François Rabelais

I drink no more than a sponge.

—François Rabelais

A quart of ale is a dish for a king.
—William Shakespeare

> He that buys land buys many stones,
> He that buys flesh buys many bones,
> He that buys eggs buys many shells,
> But he that buys good ale buys nothing else.
> —John Ray

All alcoholic drinks, rightly used, are good for body and soul alike, but as a restorative of both there is nothing like brandy.

—George Saintsbury

It is the unbroken testimony of all history that alcoholic liquors have been used by the strongest, wisest, handsomest, and in every way best races of all times.

—George Saintsbury

They speak of my drinking, but never think of my thirst.
—Scottish Proverb

I would give all my fame for a pot of ale and safety.
—William Shakespeare

Alcohol is the anesthesia by which we endure the operation of life.
—George Bernard Shaw

Gin was mother's milk to her.
—George Bernard Shaw

I hate to advocate drugs, alcohol, violence, or insanity to anyone, but they've always worked for me.
—Hunter S. Thompson

"I think this calls for a drink," has long been one of our national slogans.
—James Thurber

I'd rather have a free bottle in front of me than a prefrontal lobotomy.
—Tom Waits

Give me another drink and I'll tell you all you want to know.
—Fats Waller

A RECIPE FOR *ASSES' MILK*

Far surpasses any imitation of it that can be made. It should be milked into a glass that is kept warm by being in a basin of hot water.

The fixed air that asses' milk contains gives some people a pain in the stomach. To relieve this wind a tea-spoonful of rum may be taken with it, but this must not be added to the milk until the moment that it is swallowed.

—Maria Eliza Rundell, *A New System of Domestic Cookery; Formed upon Principles of Economy, and Adapted to the Use of Private Families* (1806)

On a dinner party he had attended:
We sat down thirty people. Few got up sober, for we were at the table and bottle seven hours and a half.

—King William IV of England

After all, the only proper intoxication is conversation.

—Oscar Wilde

> While beer brings gladness, don't forget
> That water only makes you wet.
> —Harry Leon Wilson

It was my Uncle George who discovered that alcohol was a food well in advance of modern medical thought.

—P.G. Wodehouse

To drink? Elephant beer, malty and mud brown, a liquid sensation that eclipses Fodor's ability to describe it.

—Ira Wood

The worst thing about some men is that when they are not drunk they are sober.

—William Butler Yeats

My grandmother is over 80 and still doesn't need glasses. Drinks right out of the bottle.

—Henny Youngman

LATE NIGHT
MENU

I've known what it is to be hungry, but I always went right to a restaurant.
—Ring Lardner

My mother was a recreational cook, but what she basically believed about cooking was that if you worked hard and prospered, someone else would do it for you.

—Nora Ephron

The Palm [restaurant in New York] is a joint for sadists to entertain masochists....Their steaks are often good, but the lobsters—with claws the size of Arnold Schwarzenegger's forearms—are as glazed and tough as most of the customers.

—Malcolm S. Forbes

The $100-plus dinner in New York is a major speculative undertaking akin to going after sunken treasure....the cost of the expedition is going to be steep [and] you'll come out of it enriched or just soaked.

—Ross K. Baker

The French fried potato has become an inescapable horror in almost every public eating place in the country. "French fries," say the menus, but they are not French fries any longer. They are a furry-textured substance with the taste of plastic wood.

—Russell Baker

On buying food at the Horn & Hardart Automat in 1950s New York:
I loved it. To a little kid from Istria, it was magic.

—Lidia Bastianich

"Little old lady restaurants": New York's own islands of watercress and Postum in seas of gastronomical exotica.

—Julie Baumgold

[The pub] was a revolutionary invention [and] immediately began to erode the whole traditional image of the hotel as a house.

—Mark Girouard

There is nothing which has yet been contrived by man, by which so much happiness is produced as by a good tavern or inn; a tavern chair is the home of human felicity.

—Samuel Johnson

HOW TO KEEP FRESH SALMON A WHOLE MONTH IN HIS PERFECT TASTE AND DELICACIE

First seeth your Salmon according to the usual manner, then sinke it in apt and close vessels in wine vinegar with a branch of Rosmarie therein.

By this means Vintners and Cookes may make profit thereof when it is scarce in the markets, and Salmon thus prepared may bee profitably brought out of Ireland and sold in London or elsewhere.

—Sir Hugh Platt, *Delightes for Ladies, to Adorne Their Persons, Tables, Closets, and Distillatories, With Bewties, Banquets, Perfumes, and Waters* (1600)

Inns are the mirror and at the same time the flower of a people.

—Hilaire Belloc

Toots Shor's restaurant is so crowded nobody goes there anymore.

—Yogi Berra

People are getting tired of going out to expensive restaurants and spending lots of money for seven pea pods and a two-inch steak.

—Lynne Bien

The meal was pretentious—a kind of beetroot soup with greasy *croûtons*; pork underdone with loud vulgar cabbage, potato croquettes, tinned peas in tiny jam-tart cases, watery gooseberry sauce; trifle made with a resinous wine, so jammy that all my teeth lit up at once.

—Anthony Burgess

If Broadway shows charge preview prices while the cast is in dress rehearsal, why should restaurants charge full price when their dining room and kitchen staffs are still practicing?

—Marian Burros

Catering is the cottage industry of New York. All a caterer needs is a Cuisinart, some pots and pans and a couple of food magazines to start out. They get jobs, though they don't necessarily get repeats.

—Donald Bruce White

On reducing prices during the first few weeks a new restaurant is in business:
There are always minor hiccups along the line.

—Antony Worrall-Thompson

Today's restaurant is theater on a grand scale.

—Marian Burros

A restaurant is a fantasy—a kind of living fantasy in which diners are the most important members of the cast.

—Warner LeRoy

We signal the captain, taking time out against the wall. He frowns. He groans. His feet hurt. His ulcer rages. He hates his wife. The risotto will take 25 minutes. Lasagna will take even longer.

—Gael Greene

The majority of [New York waiters] give the impression of being men who have been drafted into the job during a period of martial law and are only waiting for the end of the emergency to get back to a really congenial occupation such as slum demolition or debt collecting.

—Alan Brien

On service in London restaurants:
All that changing of plates and flapping of napkins while you wait 40 minutes for your food.

—Hugh Casson

The waitress/waiter's retort:
I've got only one other speed, and it's slower.

—anonymous

When you find a waiter who is a waiter and not an actor, writer, musician or poet, you've found a jewel.

—André Soltner

Waitresses who are tipped don't spill.

—anonymous

The haughty sommelier, with his talismanic tasting cup and sometimes irritating self-assurance, is perceived more as the high priest of some arcane rite than as a dining room functionary paid to help you enjoy the evening.

—Frank J. Prial

New York waiters, probably the surliest in the Western world...are better images of their city than that journalistic favorite—the taxi driver.

—Alan Brien

On dining at the Bronx Zoo:
At 5:30 the morning shift of commissary workers arrive to stock the coffee urns, bring in fresh food and prepare for the daylong job of feeding the humans.

—Francis X. Clines

Lyon is full of temperamental gourmets, eternally engaged in a never-ending search for that imaginary, perfect, unknown little back-street bistro, where one can dine in the style of Louis XIV for the price of a pack of peanuts.

—Roy Andries de Groot

On Alsatian restaurants:
If rich food can kill, people live dangerously here.

—Alice Furland

On the opening of Petrossian in New York, a "caviar restaurant":
Grown men have been seen fleeing after reading the menu posted outside.

—William E. Geist

Go along, go along quickly, and set all you have on the table for us. We don't want doughnuts, honey buns, poppy cakes, and other dainties; bring us a whole sheep, serve a goat and forty-year-old mead! And plenty of vodka, not vodka with all sorts of fancies, not with raisins and flavorings, but pure foaming vodka, that hisses and bubbles like mad.

—Nikolai Gogol

On the renewed popularity of roadside diners:
The diner is everybody's kitchen.

—Richard Gutman

A bill of fare with one real raisin on it instead of the word "raisin", with one real egg instead of the word "egg", might be an inadequate meal, but it would at least be a commencement of reality.

—William James

Nouvelle cuisine roughly translated means, "I can't believe I spent $96 and I'm still hungry!"

—Mike Kalina

In America, even your menus have the gift of language...."The Chef's own Vienna Roast. A hearty, rich meat loaf, gently seasoned to perfection and served in a creamy nest of mashed farm potatoes and strictly fresh garden vegetables." Of course, what you get is cole slaw and a slab of meat, but that doesn't matter because the menu has already started your juices going. Oh, those menus. In America, they are poetry.

—Laurie Lee

On the day the Biltmore Hotel's Men's Bar first admitted women:
The men were so busy looking at the women, they didn't drink.

—Hank Leslie

On eating his way through 5,000 New York City restaurants in alphabetical order:
When I was a small boy, my father told me never to recommend a church or a woman to anyone. And I have found it wise never to recommend a restaurant either. Something always goes wrong with the cheese soufflé.

—Edmund G. Love

Nobody ever escaped punishment for unrighteous treatment of a cook. That guild is sacrosanct.
—Menander

We may live without poetry, music, and art;
We may live without conscience and live without heart;
We may live without friends, we may live without books,
But civilized man cannot live without cooks.

—Owen Meredith

The disparity between a restaurant's price and the food quality rises in direct proportion to the size of the pepper mill.

—Bryan Miller

The quality of [a restaurant's] food is in inverse proportion to a dining room's altitude, especially atop bank and hotel buildings (airplanes are an extreme example).

—Bryan Miller

On John McSorley and New York's McSorley's Ale House:
He liked to get a whole onion in the hollowed out heel of a loaf of French bread and eat it as if it were an apple. He had an extraordinary appetite for onions, the stronger the better, and said that "Good ale, raw onions, and no ladies" was the motto of his saloon.

—Joseph Mitchell

Dinner at the Huntercombes' possessed only two dramatic features—the wine was a farce and the food a tragedy.

—Anthony Powell

I traveled a good deal all over the world, and I got along pretty good in all these foreign countries, for I have a theory that it's their country and they got a right to run it like they want to.

—Will Rogers

I dislike feeling at home when I am abroad.

—George Bernard Shaw

Incidentally, if you are ever in Fresno, California, you will find a large Armenian community. And in the midst of it you will find George's Restaurant. It is sort of high-tech Armenian, but George's lamb shanks should be declared a national treasure!

—Jeff Smith (The Frugal Gourmet)

He showed me his bill of fare to tempt me to dine with him. "Foh," said I, "I value not your bill of fare, give me your bill of company."

—Jonathan Swift

On nouvelle cuisine:
Each mouthful is so poignant, however, that our appetite, if not assuaged, is at least abashed. To be hungry before such food is as vulgar—as seemingly wrong—as feeling lust before the Venus de Milo.

—John Thorne

I'm in favor of liberalized immigration because of the effect it would have on restaurants. I'd let just about everybody in except the English.

—Calvin Trillin

One person cooking at home cannot pay attention to too many things. If a woman makes three dishes, she will get nervous on the first, the second will suffer and the third will be a disaster.

—René Veaux

Marriage is not merely sharing the fettucini, but sharing the burden of finding the fettucini restaurant in the first place.

—Calvin Trillin

I might glorify my bill of fare until I was tired; but after all, the Scotchman would shake his head and say, "Where's your haggis?" and the Fijian would sigh and say, "Where's your missionary?"

—Mark Twain

The Americans are the grossest feeders of any civilized nation known. As a nation, their food is heavy, coarse, and indigestible, while it is taken in the least artificial forms that cookery will allow. The predominance of grease in the American kitchen, coupled with the habits of hearty eating, and the constant expectoration, are the causes of the diseases of the stomach which are so common in America.

—James Fenimore Cooper

Though regarded with disdain by the chic, and horror by the alfalfa-sprout crowd, hot dogs are flat-out wonderful. And versatile. Dripping with hot onions and ball-park mustard from a Sabrett man, they taste like New York; served in little cardboard doo-hickeys and called frankforts, they taste like America. They also make no unreasonable demands on the home cook.

—Vladimir Estragon

You can find your way across this country using burger joints the way a navigator uses stars.

—Charles Kuralt

Around every corner lurk greasy Fisherman's Platters that give children nightmares. Naugahyde minute steaks that put tofuburgers in a favorable light and all those ubiquitous fast-food indigestion huts.

—Bryan Miller

I would rather live in Russia on black bread and vodka than in the United States at the best hotels. America knows nothing of food, love or art.

—Isadora Duncan

On the United States:
Thirty-two religions and but one course *(piat)* at dinner.

—Talleyrand

> *If you are going to America, bring food.*
> *—Fran Lebowitz*

I've run more risk in eating my way across the country than in all my driving.

—Duncan Hines

The highway is replete with culinary land mines disguised as quaint local restaurants that carry such reassuring names as Millie's, Pop's and Capt'n Dick's.

—Bryan Miller

You can travel fifty thousand miles in America without once tasting a piece of good bread.

—Henry Miller

Never eat Chinese food in Oklahoma.

—Bryan Miller

Texas does not, like any other region, simply have indigenous dishes. It proclaims them. It congratulates you on your arrival, at having escaped from the slop pails of the other 49 states.

—Alistair Cooke

A gourmet restaurant in Cincinnati is one where you leave the tray on the table after you eat.

—anonymous

Not only is New York City the nation's melting pot, it is also the casserole, the chafing dish and the charcoal grill.

—John V. Lindsay

> *There is nothing as American as*
> *a French chef from the Bronx.*
> —Susan Heller Anderson and David W. Dunlap

[W]e have learned that the Greek towns, the German towns, the China towns, the Japanese towns, the Lebanese markets, the Basque communities, all point to the fact that we get along best in America not as we are melted down but as we form a sort of stew, in which many traditions and flavors and cultures can each add to the pot, but each can be distinguished. No other nation in the world does this stew as well as we do.

—Jeff Smith (The Frugal Gourmet)

Do not accept any food from an airline that you would not accept from a vendor in Calcutta. If it's bottled or if you peel it yourself, it may be alright. Otherwise it may stay with you for the rest of your life.

—Roy G. Blount, Jr.

You learn from the elders—or by accident. The first time I picked up a taro leaf, I ate a piece and had a rash for three days!

—Amy Ferguson-Ota

No purist talk here of letting the flavors speak for themselves, the English let them sing in concert.

—Juliet Annan

There are in England sixty different religions and only one gravy, melted butter.

—Marquis Francesco Caracciolo

The most disagreeable thing at sea is the cookery; for there is not, properly speaking, any professional cook on board. The worst sailor is generally chosen for that purpose. Hence comes the proverb used among the English sailors, that "God sends meat, and the devil sends cooks."

—Benjamin Franklin

More than any other in Western Europe, Britain remains a country where a traveler...has to think twice before indulging in the ordinary food of ordinary people.

—Joseph Lelyveld

The British tourist is always happy abroad so long as the natives are waiters.

—Robert Morley

I doubt whether English cookery, for the very reason that it is so gross, is not better for man's moral and spiritual nature than French. In the former case, you know that you are gratifying your animal needs and propensities, and are duly ashamed of it; but, in dealing with these French delicacies, you delude yourself into the idea that you are cultivating your taste while filling your belly.

—Nathaniel Hawthorne

If the British can survive their meals, they can survive anything.

—George Bernard Shaw

THE FIRST RECORDED RECIPE FOR *BUBBLE AND SQUEAK*

Boil, chop, and fry it, with a little butter, pepper, and salt, some cabbage, and lay it on slices of underdone beef, lightly fried.

—Maria Eliza Rundell, *A New System of Domestic Cookery; Formed upon Principles of Economy, and Adapted to the Use of Private Families* (1806)

Anybody who minds his belly at all is nervously aware that the land is rich with regional delicacies: the jellied eels and mushy peas of the East End; the tripe and onions of the Northwest; the...Haggis and bashed neeps of Scotland; the traditional English breakfast of fatty bacon and well-greased eggs.

—The London Times

To eat figs off the tree in the very early morning, when they have been barely touched by the sun, is one of the exquisite pleasures of the Mediterranean.

—Elizabeth David

You are where you eat.

—Pamela Fiori

You can't judge Egypt by *Aïda*.

—Ronald Firbank

Reminds me of my safari in Africa. Somebody forgot the corkscrew and for several days we had to live on nothing but food and water.

—W.C. Fields

If I actually ate anything in Bombay, I don't remember it, but I seem to have absorbed a comprehensive sampling of the city's cooking by osmosis. Wherever I turned, women were preparing meager family meals over small fires of dried dung, and any passerby could "taste" the whole spectrum of Indian cookery in the normal course of respiration.

—Jay Jacobs

To this day, my first order of business in an unfamiliar town is to dog down its more obscure streets and alleys, following my nose along whatever digressive paths an intriguing odor may lead it, mingling with the street people, haunting the street markets, eating street food.

—Jay Jacobs

Nachman's Rule: When it comes to foreign food, the less authentic the better.

—Gerald Nachman

The trouble with eating Italian food is that five or six days later you're hungry again.

—George Miller

All Italy is in the fine, penetrating smell; and all Provence; and all Spain. An onion- or garlic-scented atmosphere hovers alike over the narrow calli of Venice, the cool courts of Cordova, and the thronged amphitheatre of Arles. It is the only atmosphere breathed by the Latin peoples of the South, so that ever it must suggest blue skies and endless sunshine, cypress groves and olive orchards. For the traveller it is interwoven with memories of the golden canvases of Titian, the song of Dante, the music of Mascagni.

—Elizabeth Pennell

On travelling in the Soviet Union and ordering breakfast:
So in our pride we ordered for breakfast, an omelet, toast and coffee and what has just arrived is a tomato salad with onions, a dish of pickles, a big slice of watermelon and two bottles of cream soda.

—John Steinbeck

I can't believe I ate the whole thing.®

Plop plop, fizz fizz, oh what a relief it is!®

> —Advertisements for Alka-Seltzer,™ added to water to create a potent potable for the relief of indigestion and stomach acid

---

BEFORE THERE WAS BROMO...

Wind colic is promptly relieved by peppermint essence taken in a little warm water....

Sickness of the stomach is most promptly relieved by drinking a teacupful of hot soda and water. If it brings the offending matter up, all the better.

A teaspoonful of ground mustard in a cupful of warm water is a prompt and reliable emetic, and should be resorted to in cases of poisoning or cramps in the stomach from over-eating.

—Hugo Ziemann, Steward of the White House, and Mrs. F.L. Gillette, *The Original White House Cookbook: Contains Cooking, Toilet and Household Recipes, Menus, Dinner-giving, Table Etiquette, Care of the Sick, Health Suggestions, Facts Worth Knowing, etc.* (1887)

One reason I don't drink is that I want to know when I am having a good time.
—Lady Nancy Astor

Total abstinence is easier for me than perfect moderation.
—Saint Augustine

Drunkenness is the ruin of reason. It is premature old age. It is temporary death.
—Saint Basil

Let us eat and drink; for tomorrow we shall die.
—The Bible

Indigestion: A disease which the patient and his friends frequently mistake for deep religious conviction and concern for the salvation of mankind.
—Ambrose Bierce

O gluttony, it is to thee we owe our griefs!
—Geoffrey Chaucer

Life itself is the proper binge.
—Julia Child

For a bad hangover take the juice of two quarts of whiskey.

—Eddie Condon

Gluttony is an emotional escape, a sign that something is eating us.

—Peter De Vries

"I feel a very unusual sensation," said Mr. St. Barbe, after dining with Neufchatels. "If it's not indigestion, I think it must be gratitude."

—Benjamin Disraeli

Sir Osbert once recalled that while he was attending Eton a classmate committed suicide. At the memorial service, the headmaster asked the boys whether they could give any hint as to why so well-liked and highly regarded a lad should have done away with himself. A moment of silence. Then the proverbial boy in the back timidly waved his hand: "Do you suppose, sir, it might have been the food?"

—Willard R. Espy

'Twas a woman who drove me to drink, and I never had the courtesy to thank her for it.

—W.C. Fields

The cold truth is that family dinners are more often than not an ordeal of nervous indigestion, preceded by hidden resentment and ennui and accompanied by psychosomatic jitters.

—M.F.K. Fisher

Nature will castigate those who don't masticate.

—Horace Fletcher

The spirit cannot endure the body when overfed but, if underfed, the body cannot endure the spirit.

—Saint Francis de Sales

Eat not to dullness. Drink not to elevation.

—Benjamin Franklin

I saw few die of hunger, of eating—100,000.

—Benjamin Franklin

In general, mankind, since the improvement of cookery, eats twice as much as nature requires.

—Benjamin Franklin

Three good meals a day is bad living.

—Benjamin Franklin

A drinker has a hole under his nose that all his money runs into.

—Thomas Fuller

A gourmet is just a glutton with brains.

—Phillip W. Haberman, Jr.

I entered the drinking life long before I had my first sip of alcohol....In my young life, drinking was everywhere, from the neighborhood bars to the furtive bushes of summer camp. Even the comic books taught their indirect lessons: A magic potion could transform the shiest, weakest boy into Captain America or the Blue Beetle. Drinking, in short, was an integral part of my life.

—Pete Hamill

APICIUS: NAME YOUR POISON

Marcus Gavius Apicius was one of the earliest authors of books on cookery. He lived in Rome during the first years of Christianity and the reign of the Roman Emperor Tiberius. Hardly a role model for modern cookbook authors and gourmets, Apicius was a glutton and hedonist of the highest order.

Seneca recorded his death, noting that he committed suicide by poison when, upon awakening with a hangover after a bacchanalian food/sex/wine-fest, he was heartbroken to find he had spent most of his fortune. A true gourmand, he decided that life was not worth living if it could not be done in the grand style to which he had become accustomed.

Indigestion is an excellent commonplace for two people that have never met before.

—William Hazlitt

My soul is dark with stormy riot,
Directly traceable to diet.
—Samuel Hoffenstein

Most people eat as though they were fattening themselves for market.

—E.W. Howe

Indigestion is charged by God with enforcing morality on the stomach.

—Victor Hugo

Abstinence is as easy to me as temperance would be difficult.

—Samuel Johnson

Drinking may be practised with great prudence; a man who exposes himself when he is intoxicated has not the art of getting drunk.

—Samuel Johnson

If we heard it said of Orientals that they habitually drank liquor which went to their heads, deprived them of reason and made them vomit, we should say: "How very barbarous!"

—La Bruyère

A man takes a drink, the drink takes another, and the drink takes the man.
—Sinclair Lewis

A man who is rich in his adolescence is almost doomed to be a dilettante at table.
—A.J. Liebling

Short-term amnesia is not the worst affliction if you have an Irish flair for the sauce.
—Norman Mailer

If you drink, don't drive. Don't even putt.
—Dean Martin

I haven't touched a drop of alcohol since the invention of the funnel.
—Malachy McCourt

The young don't drink so much these days. In my day they were always throwing up in their top hats.
—Alice-Leone Moats

Roumanian-Yiddish cooking has killed more Jews than Hitler.
—Zero Mostel

What suffering results from over-eating! Let man, then, drive from his heart and from his hand the idleness which finds its delights in blamable pleasures and cleave to moderation when he eats...for there are many among men who fail to hold the reins taut, but let them drop loosely upon their bellies.

—Oppian

More people are killed by over-eating and drinking than by the sword.

—Sir William Osler

Not drunk is he who from the floor
Can rise alone and still drink more;
But drunk is he who prostrate lies
Without the power to move or rise.

—Thomas Love Peacock

The recipes of cookery are swelled to a volume; but a good stomach excels them all.

—William Penn

Peter was ill during the evening, on consequence of overeating himself. His mother put him to bed and gave him a dose of camomile tea, but Flopsy, Mopsy and Cottontail had bread and milk and blackberries for supper.

—Beatrix Potter

Satiety is a neighbor to continued pleasures.

—Quintilian

When belly with bad pains doth swell,
It matters nought what else goes well.
—Sadi

Pride may be allowed to this or that degree, else a man cannot keep up his dignity. In gluttony there must be eating, in drunkenness there must be drinking: 'tis not the eating, nor 'tis not the drinking that is to be blamed, but the excess. So with pride.

—John Selden

What is nourishment to a hungry man becomes a burden
to a full stomach.
—Seneca

Things sweet to taste prove in digestion sour.

—William Shakespeare

Unquiet meals make ill digestions.

—William Shakespeare

I have heard it remarked by a statesman of high reputation, that most great men have died of over-eating themselves.

—Sir Henry Taylor

He who distinguishes the true savor of his food can never be a glutton; he who does not cannot be otherwise.

—Henry David Thoreau

A fool that eats till he is sick must fast till he is well.

—George Walter Thornbury

TOUCHÉ

Among British society's greatest odd couples was George Bernard Shaw and G.K. Chesterton. Although great friends the two men were even greater opposites. Shaw was quiet, sardonic, unconventional, a vegetarian, and thin as a rail. Chesterton was loud, argumentative, traditional, and a hearty meat-eater, and obese. Neither could resist poking fun at whatever was available, including each other.

Once, while dining together in public, Chesterton couldn't help remarking on Shaw's thin figure, "Looking at you, Shaw, people would think there was a famine in England."

Turning to his large companion, Shaw retorted, "And looking at you, Chesterton, people would think you were the cause of it."

There is no question that Rumanian-Jewish food is heavy. One meal is equal in heaviness, I would guess, to eight or nine years of steady mung-bean eating. Following the Rumanian tradition, garlic is used in excess to keep the vampires away; following the Jewish tradition, a dispenser of schmaltz (liquid chicken fat) is kept on the table to give vampires heartburn if they get through the garlic defense.

—Calvin Trillin

Part of the secret of success in life is to eat what you like and let the food fight it out inside.

—Mark Twain

Sometimes too much to drink is barely enough.

—Mark Twain

Water, taken in moderation, cannot hurt anybody.

—Mark Twain

The mind of most scientists is like a glutton with poor digestion.

—Vauvenargues

On Christian Dior:
Poor, darling fellow—he *died* of food. He was killed by the dinner table.

—Diana Vreeland

Enough is as good as a meal.

—Oscar Wilde

Too many cooks spoil the brothel.

—Polly Adler

In Port Headland [Australia], happiness comes smithereen-shaped.

—Jonathan Aitken

Zee always went naked in the house, except for the brassiere she wore when it was her turn to get dinner. Once, cooking French-fried potatoes in a kettle of boiling fat, she had come within an inch of crisping her most striking features.

—G.S. Albee

Try to cook so that it will surprise a little, agreeably...and astonish slightly, without shocking.

—Jean Marie Amat

An Irishman is the only man in the world who will step over the bodies of a dozen naked women to get to a bottle of stout.

—anonymous

> Heavenly Father, bless us,
> And keep us all alive,
> There's ten of us to dinner
> And not enough for five.
> —anonymous

SAY NO TO SECONDS

Never ask to be helped to soup a second time. The hostess may ask you to take a second plate, but you will politely decline. Fish chowder, which is served in soup plates, is said to be an exception which proves this rule, and when eating of that it is correct to take a second plateful if desired.

—Hugo Ziemann, Steward of the White House, and Mrs. F.L. Gillette, *The Original White House Cookbook: Contains Cooking, Toilet and Household Recipes, Menus, Dinner-giving, Table Etiquette, Care of the Sick, Health Suggestions, Facts Worth Knowing, etc.* (1887)

What should we be without our meals? They come to us in our joys and sorrows and are the most blessed break that dullness can ever know.

—anonymous

The trouble with most cookbooks is that they assume that people live the way they don't live.

—Mrs. Appleyard

Murder is commoner among cooks than among members of any other profession.

—W.H. Auden

The joys of the table are superior to all other pleasures, notably those of personal adornment, of drinking and of love, and those procured by perfumes and by music.

—Hassan El Baghadadi

Jewish cuisine differs from that of my father's in both philosophy and content, but in its preoccupation with food as a gesture of love, the two have much in common. If the price we pay for that gesture be a little pain in the night, a little agony on the bathroom scales, a prowl down dark corridors groping for the Bisodol*—well, who said love was all roses without a thorn?

—Russell Baker

[*Bisodol is an antacid.]

The refectory is a cenacle in which the taking of food is transfigured almost into a sacrament.

—Monica Baldwin

I was raised in a world where food was the center of life, where everyone's labor and activity centered on the feeding of the family.

—Lidia Bastianich

After a perfect meal we are more susceptible to the ecstasy of love than at any other time.
—Dr. Hans Bazli

I don't like gourmet cooking of "this" cooking or "that" cooking. I like *good* cooking.

—James Beard

The word "gourmet" has been run into the ground. Anybody's cousin who drinks wine with his meals, or who substitutes broccoli for potatoes considers himself a gourmet. It's become a dreaded word in the American language.

—James Beard

I have always thought that there is no more fruitful source of family discontent than badly cooked dinners and untidy ways.

—Mrs. Isabella Beeton

On living in Dublin in the 1930s:
To get enough to eat was regarded as an achievement. To get drunk was a victory.

—Brendan Behan

The true gourmet, like the true artist, is one of the unhappiest creatures existent. His trouble comes from so seldom finding what he constantly seeks: perfection.

—Ludwig Bemelmans

A Recipe for *Indian Slapjack*

To one quart of milk, add 1 pint of Indian meal, stirring well. Add 4 whole eggs, well beaten, 4 spoons of flour, a little salt. Beat all together. Bake on griddles, or fry in a dry pan. May also be baked in a pan which has been rubbed with suet, lard or butter.

—Amelia Simmons, *American Cookery; or, The Art of Dressing Viands, Fish, Poultry and Vegetables, and the Best Modes of Making Pastes, Puffs, Pies, Tarts, Puddings, Custards and Preserves, and all Kinds of Cakes, from the Imperial Plumb to Plain Cake* (1796)

Cantonese will eat anything in the sky but airplanes, anything in the sea but submarines and anything with four legs but the table.

—Amanda Bennett

On gatherings in London's financial district:
Silver and ermine and red faces full of port wine.

—John Betjeman

Better is the life of a poor man in a cottage...than delicate fare in another man's house; and better a dry morsel and quietness therewith, than a house full of sacrifices and strife.

—The Bible

Every man should eat and drink, and enjoy the good of all his labour, it is the gift of God.

—The Bible

A kiss is but a modified bite, and a fond mother, when she says her babe is "almost good enough to eat", merely shows that she is herself only a trifle too good to eat it.

—Ambrose Bierce

Connoisseur: A specialist who knows everything about something and nothing about anything else.

—Ambrose Bierce

Digestion: The conversion of victuals into virtues.

—Ambrose Bierce

Epicure: An opponent of Epicurus, an abstemious philosopher who, holding that pleasure should be the chief aim of man, wasted no time in gratification of the senses.

—Ambrose Bierce

Friendship is like earthenware, once broken it can be mended.

—Josh Billings

I hated myself because I smelt of onions and meat, and I seriously considered suicide in the cistern which supplied the house.

—Louise De Koven Bowen

Anybody who eats three meals a day should understand why cookbooks outsell sex books three to one.

—L.M. Boyd

Gazing at the typewriter in moments of desperation, I console myself with three thoughts: alcohol at six, dinner at eight and to be immortal you've got to be dead.

—Gyles Brandeth

Grub first, then ethics.

—Bertolt Brecht

For unknown foods, the nose acts always as a sentinel and cries, "Who goes there?"

—Brillat-Savarin

He who wants to eat cannot sleep.

—Brillat-Savarin

The discovery of a new dish does more for a man than the discovery of a star.

—Brillat-Savarin

There are only two questions to ask me about food. Is it good? And is it authentic? We are open [to] new ideas, but not if it means destroying our history. And food is history.

—Giuliano Bugialli

Imagine, if you can, what the rest of the evening was like. How they crouched by the fire which blazed and leaped and made much of itself in the little grate. How they removed the covers of the dishes, and found rich, hot savory soup, which was a meal in itself, and sandwiches and toast and muffins enough for both of them.

—Frances Hodgson Burnett

Cookery has become an art, a noble science; cooks are gentlemen.

—Robert Burton

One's stomach is one's internal environment.

—Samuel Butler

As I drove in she was walking into the house with eggs for breakfast and homemade biscuits ready for baking. Somehow in rural Southern culture, food is always the first thought of neighbors when there is trouble. That is something they can do and not feel uncomfortable. It is something they do not have to explain or discuss or feel self-conscious about. "Here I brought you some fresh eggs for your breakfast. And here's a cake. And some potato salad." It means, "I love you. And I am sorry for what you are going through and I will share as much of your burden as I can." And maybe potato salad is a better way of saying it.

—Will D. Campbell

WAYS TO DRESS EGGS

Excepting meat, nothing furnishes a greater variety in the kitchen than eggs; but before I proceed to the various ways of dressing them, I shall speak of their utility. The yolks of new-laid eggs beat up in warm water, is called hen's milk, and, taken going to bed, is good for a cold. The fine skin within the shell, beat and mixed with the white, is excellent for chapped lips.

The shell, burnt and pounded, will whiten the teeth: taken in wine, it is good for stopping a spitting of blood.

—Francis Collingwood and John Wollams, "principal Cooks at the Crown & Anchor Tavern in the Strand", *The French Family Cook,* translated by the authors from their original French edition into English (1793)

Give us this day our daily taste. Restore to us soups that spoons will not sink in and sauces which are never the same twice. Raise up among us stews with more gravy than we have bread to blot it with...Give us pasta with a hundred fillings.

—Robert Farrar Capon

I like a cook who smiles out loud when he tastes his own work. Let God worry about your modesty; I want to see your enthusiasm.

—Robert Farrar Capon

No artist can work simply for results; he must also *like* the work of getting them. Not that there isn't a lot of drudgery in any art—and more in cooking than in most—but that if a man has never been pleasantly surprised at the way the custard sets or flour thickens, there is not much hope of making a cook of him.

—Robert Farrar Capon

We had the first of a very relaxed and informal series of meals with our family. Earlier, when Rosalynn was visiting the White House, some of our staff asked the chef and cooks if they thought they could prepare the kind of meals which we enjoyed in the South, and the cook said, "Yes, Ma'am, we've been fixing that kind of food for the servants for a long time."

—James E. (Jimmy) Carter

It is a difficult matter, my fellow citizens, to argue with a belly, since it has no ears.

—Marcus Cato

The belly carries the legs, and not the legs the belly.

—Cervantes

The majority of those who put together collections of verses or epigrams resemble those who eat cherries or oysters; they begin by choosing the best and end by eating everything.

—Chamfort

I am such a great connoisseur that I can tell the difference between the tang of the Beaverbrook *Daily Express* and the mellow flavor of the *Times*.

—Arthur Joseph Champion (Lord Champion of Pontypridd)

They ate frozen meat, frozen fried potatoes and frozen peas. Blindfolded, one could not have identified the peas, and the only flavor the potatoes had was the flavor of soap. It was the monotonous fare of the besieged...but...where was the enemy?

—John Cheever

It is not greedy to enjoy a good dinner, any more than it is greedy to enjoy a good concert. But I do think there is something greedy about trying to enjoy the concert and dinner at the same time.

—G.K. Chesterton

I was 32 when I started cooking; up until then, I just ate.

—Julia Child

Upon being asked if her husband liked her cooking:
I wouldn't keep him around long if I didn't feed him well.

—Julia Child

In France, cooking is a serious art form and a national sport.

—Julia Child

A well-filled stomach is indeed a great thing:
all else is luxury of life.
—Chinese Proverb

On nouvelle cuisine:
It's so beautifully arranged on the plate—you know someone's fingers have been all over it.

—Julia Child

Noncooks think it's silly to invest two hours' work in two minutes' enjoyment; but if cooking is evanescent, well, so is the ballet.

—Julia Child

Today, in the 1990s, the culinary arts have become a respected profession, and many of our chefs have university degrees. It is even possible to study for a master's degree in gastronomy. And about time, I say.

—Julia Child

> ### THERE IS NO FINER INVESTMENT FOR ANY COMMUNITY THAN PUTTING MILK INTO BABIES.
> ### —WINSTON S. CHURCHILL

When one wakes up after daylight one should breakfast; five hours after that, luncheon. Six hours after luncheon, dinner. Thus one becomes independent of the sun, which otherwise meddles too much in one's affairs and upsets the routine of work.

—Winston S. Churchill

[James Beard] was an innovator, an experimenter, a missionary in bringing the gospel of good cooking to the home table.

—Craig Claiborne

A transgression, a crime, entering a man's existence, eats it up like a malignant growth, consumes it like a fever.

—Joseph Conrad

Recipes are like poems; they keep what kept us. And good cooks are like poets; they know how to count.

—Henri Coulette

I never see an egg brought on my table but I feel penetrated with the wonderful change it would have undergone but for my gluttony; it might have been a gentle, useful hen, leading her chickens with a care and vigilance which speaks shame to many women.

—St. John de Crèvecoeur

When I was a student I was always on a tight budget. I wanted to be able to go to a restaurant and order without looking at the prices on the menu.

—Michael Crichton

Some people have food, but no appetite; others have an appetite, but no food. I have both. The Lord be praised.

—Oliver Cromwell

When I was young and poor, my favorite dish was caviar accompanied by a half bottle of Bollinger. But repetition destroys any pleasure, gastronomic or sexual, and now I have no favorite dish having eliminated all my "favorites"! Now I like nothing better than a bowl of well-made Scottish porridge, accompanied by a glass of good sweet milk, "supped" in spoonfuls in turn. Delicious, good and nourishing and without after-effects.

—A.J. Cronin

Cuisine is when things taste like themselves.

—Curnonsky

In cooking, as in all the arts, simplicity is the sign of perfection.

—Curnonsky

Describing the sights taken in by little Veruca Salt on her way down the garbage chute in Willy Wonka's chocolate factory:

> And then, a little further down
> A mass of others gather round:
> A bacon rind, some rancid lard,
> A loaf of bread gone stale and hard,
> A steak that nobody could chew,
> An oyster from an oyster stew,
> Some liverwurst so old and gray,
> One smelled it from a mile away,
> A rotten nut, a reeky pear,
> A thing the cat left on the stair.
>
> —Roald Dahl

It is odd how all men develop the notion, as they grow older, that their mothers were wonderful cooks. I have yet to meet a man who will admit that his mother was a kitchen assassin and nearly poisoned him.

—Robertson Davies

Good painting is like good cooking—it can be tasted, but not explained.

—Maurice de Vlaminck

Food is to eat, not to frame and hang on the wall.

—William Denton

Oliver Twist had asked for more.

—Charles Dickens

TO SAVE POTTED BIRDS THAT BEGIN TO BE BAD

I have seen potted Birds, which have come a great way, often smell so bad, that nobody could bear the Smell for the rankness of the Butter. By managing them in the following manner, I have made them as good as ever was eat.

Set a large Sauce-pan of clean Water on the Fire. When it boils, take off the Butter at the Top, then take the Fowls out one by one, throw them into the Sauce-pan of Water half a minute, whip them out, and dry them on a clean Cloth inside and out. So do all till they are quite done. Scald the pot clean. When the Birds are quite cool, season them with Mace, Pepper, and Salt to your mind. Put them close down in the Pot, and pour clarified Butter over them.

—Mrs. Hannah Glasse, *The Art of Cookery made Plain and Easy* (1747; First cookbook written in English by a woman to have achieved any notoriety—was a bestseller in Great Britain for almost 100 years.)

When you don't have any money, the problem is food. When you have money, it's sex. When you have both, it's health.

—J.P. Donleavy

On presidential parties for the press:
Wooing the press, as [George] Bush found out, is an exercise roughly akin to picnicking with a tiger. You might enjoy the meal, but the tiger always eats last.

—Maureen Dowd

Before I was born my mother was in great agony of spirit and in a tragic situation. She could take no food except iced oysters and champagne. If people ask me when I began to dance, I reply, "In my mother's womb, probably as a result of the oysters and champagne—the food of Aphrodite."

—Isadora Duncan

An empty stomach is not a good political advisor.

—Albert Einstein

No man can be wise on an empty stomach.

—George Eliot (Marian Evans Cross)

Good oil, like good wine, is a gift from the gods. The grape and the olive are among the priceless benefactions of the soil, and were destined, each in its way, to promote the welfare of man.

—George Ellwanger

There is always a best way of doing everything, if it be to boil an egg.

—Ralph Waldo Emerson

We boil at different degrees.

—Ralph Waldo Emerson

Anyone who believes for one second that the nouvelle cuisine has had any impact on the way Americans eat in their homes is crazy. It has nothing to do with anyone except possibly ten people who have chefs and are silly enough to think raspberries go with meat and kiwi with shrimp.

—Nora Ephron

Men cook more, and we all know why. It is the only interesting household task. Getting down and scrubbing the floor is done by women, or by the women they've hired.

—Nora Ephron

Whenever I get married, I start buying *Gourmet* magazine.

—Nora Ephron

Food to a large extent is what holds a society together and eating is closely linked to deep spiritual experiences.

—Peter Farb and George Armelagos

The way to a man's heart is through his stomach.

—Fanny Fern

Almost every person has something secret he likes to eat.

—M.F.K. Fisher

Probably one of the most private things in the world is an egg until it is broken.

—M.F.K. Fisher

When a man is small, he loves and hates food with a ferocity which soon dims. But at six years old his very bowels will heave when such a dish as creamed carrots or cold tapioca appears before him. His throat will close, and spots of nausea and rage swim in his vision. It is hard, later, to remember why, but at the time there is no pose in his disgust. He cannot eat; he says, "To hell with it!"

—M.F.K. Fisher

It is a delicious thing to write.

—Gustave Flaubert

Eating and sleeping are a waste of time.

—Gerald R. Ford

Life is not a spectacle or a feast; it is a predicament.

—Anatole France

The truth is that life is delicious, horrible, charming, frightful, sweet, bitter, and that it is everything.

—Anatole France

A full Belly is the Mother of all Evil.

—Benjamin Franklin

A full belly makes a dull brain.

—Benjamin Franklin

> Gourmets dig their graves with their teeth.
> —French Proverb

There is one thing more exasperating than a wife who can cook and won't and that's a wife who can't cook and will.

—Robert Frost

A belly full of gluttony will never study willingly.

—Thomas Fuller

Your belly will never let your back be warm.

—Thomas Fuller

> Philosopher, whom dost thou most affect,
> Stoics austere, or Epicurus' sect?
> Friend, 'tis my grave infrangible design
> With those to study and with these to dine.
> —Richard Garnett

Many excellent cooks are spoiled by going into the arts.

—Paul Gauguin

No mean woman can cook well, for it calls for a light head, a generous spirit, and a large heart.

—Paul Gauguin

You cannot feed the hungry on statistics.

—David Lloyd George

|||||||||||||||||||||||||||||||||||||||||||||||||||||||||||||||||||||||||||||||||

RECIPE FOR *FISH BAKED IN ASHES*

No cheese, no nonsense! Just place it tenderly in fig leaves and tie them on top with a string; then push it under hot ashes, be thinking thee wisely of the time when it is done, and burn it not up.

—Archestratus

It isn't so much what's on the table that matters, as what's on the chairs.

—W.S. Gilbert

On inventing the grocery cart:
[Customers] had a tendency to stop shopping when the baskets became too full or too heavy.

—Sylvan N. Goldman

For everyone doing rustic food, there are others out there braiding chives.

—Joyce Goldstein

The vilest of beasts is the belly.

—Greek Proverb

When we decode a cookbook, every one of us is a practicing chemist. Cooking is really the oldest, most basic application of physical and chemical forces to natural materials.

—Arthur E. Grosser

On working with actor, Debra Winger, in the film A Dangerous Woman:
Working with her wasn't like eating dessert—it was a full meal. And I would do it again in a second.

—Stephen Gyllenhaal

The readers and the hearers like my books,
But yet some writers cannot them digest;
But what care I? for when I make a feast
I would my guests should praise it, not the cooks.
—Sir John Harington

Lazy fokes' stummucks don't git tired.
—Joel Chandler Harris

Cooking in all its branches should be studied as a science, and not be looked upon as a haphazard mode of getting through life.
—Lafcadio Hearn

A full belly neither fights nor flies well.

—George Herbert

The eye is bigger then the belly.

—George Herbert

'Tis not the food, but the content,
That makes the table's merriment.
—Robert Herrick

The poor seek food, the rich seek an appetite.

—Hindi Proverb

More people will die from hit-or-miss eating than from hit-and-run driving.

—Duncan Hines

I bid myself accept the common lot; an adequate vitality would say daily: "God—what a good sleep I've had." "My eye, that was a dinner." "Now for a rattling walk,"—in short, realize life as an end in itself.

—Oliver Wendell Holmes, Jr.

In order to know whether a human being is young or old, offer it food of different kinds at short intervals. If young, it will eat anything at any hour of the day or night.

—Oliver Wendell Holmes, Sr.

> Nothing more shameless is than Appetite,
> Who still, whatever anguish load our breast,
> Makes us remember in our despite
> Both food and drink.

—Homer

Seek an appetite by hard toil.

—Horace

If you are ever at a loss to support a flagging conversation, introduce the subject of eating.

—Leigh Hunt

Laughter is brightest where food is best.

—Irish Proverb

Eggs of an hour, bread of a day, wine of a year, a friend of thirty years.

—Italian Proverb

Even old boot tastes good if it is cooked over charcoal.

—Italian Proverb

Except in the case of *Homo sapiens,* the vocation of all living creatures is eating.

—Jay Jacobs

A cookbook review:
The tome was a backbreaking thousand-odd pages thick and generously larded with color plates of presumably edible rococo and byzantine ornamentation, any subject of which would have taken a fairly accomplished home cook, working with tweezers and magnifying glass, a month to replicate.

—Jay Jacobs

The olive tree is surely the richest gift in Heaven. I can scarcely expect bread.

—Thomas Jefferson

The greatest animal in creation, the animal who cooks.

—Douglas Jerrold

TO KEEP MEAT FROM FLIES

Put in sacks, with enough straw around it so flies cannot reach through. Three-fourths of a yard or near-wide muslin is the right size for the sack. Put a little straw in the bottom, then put in the ham and lay straw in all around it; tie it tightly and hang it in a cool, dry place. Be sure the straw is all around the meat, so the flies cannot reach through to deposit the eggs. (The sacking must be done early in the season before the fly appears.)

—Hugo Ziemann, Steward of the White House, and Mrs. F.L. Gillette, *The Original White House Cookbook: Contains Cooking, Toilet and Household Recipes, Menus, Dinner-giving, Table Etiquette, Care of the Sick, Health Suggestions, Facts Worth Knowing, etc.* (1887)

You better come in my kitchen
'Cause it's going to be raining outdoors.

—Robert Johnson

A master cook! why he's the man of men,
For a professor; he designs, he draws,
He paints, he carves, he builds, he fortifies,
Makes citadels of curious fowl and fish.
Some he dry-ditches, some moats round with broths,
Mounts marrow-bones, cuts fifty angled custards,
Rears bulwark pies; and for his outer works,
He raiseth ramparts of immortal crust,
And teacheth all the tactics at one dinner—
What ranks, what files to put his dishes in,
The whole art military!

—Ben Jonson

I hate tomato roses, parsley on plates where no one will ever eat it, and
any food gotten up to look like something else.

—Barbara Kafka

O poor immortal comforts: fish, some bread and wine.

—Nikos Kazantzakis

It is the aroma that fills the space between the plate and your head. In the
apparent emptiness wafts most of the real art of cooking. Just hold your
nose and eat and you'll see how vital aromas are!

—Graham Kerr

Happiness is a Chinese meal; sorrow is a nourishment forever.
—Carolyn Kizer

Nobody can really taste food unless he's had a good look at it first.
—Alan Koehler

He who eats for two must work for three.
—Kurdish Proverb

The art of using up leftovers is not to be considered as the summit of culinary achievement.
—*Larousse Gastronomique*

"There's no such thing as bad food," Mama used to say. "There are only spoiled-rotten children."
—Sam Levenson

A good meal in troubled times is always that much salvaged from disaster.
—A.J. Liebling

An Englishman teaching an American about food is like the blind leading the one-eyed.
—A.J. Liebling

I use the verb "to eat" here to denote a selective activity, as opposed to the passive acceptance and regular renewal of nourishment, learned in infancy. An automobile receiving fuel at a filling station or an infant at the breast cannot be said to eat, nor can a number of people at any time in their lives.

—A.J. Liebling

In learning to eat, as in psychoanalysis, the customer, in order to profit, must be sensible of the cost.

—A.J. Liebling

Like most fine cooks, M. Buillon flew into rages and wept easily; the heat of kitchens perhaps affects cooks' tear ducts as well as their tempers.

—A.J. Liebling

> *The primary requisite for writing well about food is a good appetite.*
> *—A.J. Liebling*

After many banquets, then you have comforting *congee* with salty pickles—one mouthful *congee*, one little mouthful of salt pickle, just like tea and toast to you. If there is sickness, some chicken goes in, but there should be no fat in comforting food because it sits badly in the stomach.

—Florence Lin

Given extensive leisure, what do not the Chinese do? They eat crabs, drink tea, taste spring water, sing operatic airs, fly kites, play shuttle-cock, match grass blades, make paper boxes, solve complicated wire puzzles, play majong, gamble and pawn clothing, stew ginseng, watch cock-fights, romp with their children, water flowers, plant vegetables, graft fruits, play chess, take baths, hold conversations, keep cagebirds, take afternoon naps, have three meals in one, guess fingers, play at palmistry, gossip about fox spirits, go to operas, beat drums and gongs, play the flute, practise calligraphy, munch duck gizzards, salt carrots, fondle walnuts, fly eagles, feed carrier pigeons, quarrel with their tailors, go on pilgrimages, visit temples, climb mountains, watch boat races, hold bull fights, take aphrodisiacs, smoke opium, gather at street corners, shout at aeroplanes, fulminate against the Japanese, wonder at the white people, criticize their politicians, read Buddhist classics, practise deep-breathing, hold Buddhist séances, consult fortune tellers, catch crickets, eat melon seeds, gamble for moon cakes, hold lantern competitions, burn rare incense, eat noodles, solve literary riddles, train pot-flowers, send one another birthday presents, kow-tow to one another, produce children, and sleep.

—Lin Yutang

Happiness for me is largely a matter of digestion.

—Lin Yutang

If a man will be sensible and one fine morning, while he is lying in bed, count at the tips of his fingers how many things in his life truly give him enjoyment, invariably he will find food is the first one.

—Lin Yutang

What is patriotism but the love of good things we ate in our childhood.

—Lin Yutang

All's well that ends with a good meal.

—Arnold Lobel

A RECIPE FOR *ELECTION CAKE*

Three cups milk, two cups sugar, one cup yeast; stir to a batter and let stand over night; in the morning add two cups sugar, two cups butter, three eggs, half a nutmeg, one tablespoon cinnamon, one pound raisins, one gill of brandy.

Brown sugar is much better than white for this kind of cake, and it is improved by dissolving a half-teaspoonful of soda in a tablespoonful of milk in the morning. It should stand in the greased pans and rise some time until quite light before baking.

—Hugo Ziemann, Steward of the White House, and Mrs. F.L. Gillette, *The Original White House Cookbook: Contains Cooking, Toilet and Household Recipes, Menus, Dinner-giving, Table Etiquette, Care of the Sick, Health Suggestions, Facts Worth Knowing, etc.* (1887)

When you came, you were like red wine and honey,
And the taste of you burnt my mouth with its sweetness.
Now you are like morning bread,
Smooth and pleasant.
I hardly taste you at all, for I know your savor;
But I am completely nourished.

—Amy Lowell

What is food to one may be fierce poison to others.

—Lucretius

If you haven't paid the real wages of love or courage or abstention or discipline or sacrifice or wit in the eye of danger, then taking a psychedelic drug is living the life of a parasite; it's drawing on the sweets you have not earned.

—Norman Mailer

Now hopping-john was F. Jasmine's very favorite food. She had always warned them to wave a plate of rice and peas before her nose when she was in her coffin, to make certain there was no mistake; for if a breath of life was left in her, she would sit up and eat, but if she smelled the hopping-john, and did not stir, then they could just nail down the coffin and be certain she was truly dead.

—Carson McCullers

We are here and it is now. Further than that all human knowledge is moonshine.

—H.L. Mencken

Vasari, in his *Lives of the Painters*, describes how Piero di Cosimo, finding that eating interfered with his work, took to living entirely on hard-boiled eggs. He cooked these a hundred at a time, and kept a basketful beside his easel. That is one way of simplifying the pursuit of beauty.

—Aubrey Menen

Kissing don't last: cookery do.

—George Meredith

Anybody can make you enjoy the first bite of a dish, but only a real chef can make you enjoy the last.

—François Minot

Scarlett O'Hara:
As God is my witness, as God is my witness...I'm never going to be hungry again. No, nor any of my folks. If I have to steal or kill—as God is my witness, I'm never going to be hungry again.

—Margaret Mitchell

A gourmet is a being pleasing to heaven.

—Charles Monselet

A true gastronome should always be ready to eat, just as a soldier should always be ready to fight.

—Charles Monselet

I have always thought geniuses much inferior to the plain sense of the cookmaid, who can make a good pudding and keep the kitchen in order.
—Mary Wortley Montagu

> He had a broad face and a little round belly,
> That shook when he laughed like a bowlful of jelly.
> —Clement Clarke Moore

If food is poetry, is not poetry also food?
–Joyce Carol Oates

For those of you who like to scarf your popcorn in the sack, the good news is that *Newman's Own* contains an aphrodisiac.

—Paul Newman

Bad cooks—and the utter lack of reason in the kitchen—have delayed human development longest and impaired it most.

—Friedrich Nietzsche

Routine in cuisine is a crime.

—Édouard Nignon

M. Bourgignon, our "chef saucier", told me that by the time a chef is forty he is either dead or crazy.

—David Ogilvy

Man should go out of this world as he came in—chiefly on milk.

—Sir William Osler

The belly is not filled with fair words.
—François Rabelais

It is dazzling to discover smorgasbord at a South Carolina inn or a caesar salad in Arkansas. Surely, we think, such internationalism is a good sign, rather like the Daughters of the American Revolution voting for an increase in foreign aid.

—Eleanor Perenyi

I never see any home cooking. All I get is fancy stuff.

—Prince Philip, Duke of Edinburgh

I always try to make every meal *une petite merveille* (a little marvel).

—Fernand Point

To the old saying that man built the house but woman made of it a "home" might be added the modern supplement that woman accepted cooking as a chore but man has made it a recreation.

—Emily Post

Men make better cooks than women because they put so much more feeling into it.

—Myrtle Reed

Never eat tomorrow what you can manage to eat today. A meal saved is a meal turned bad. It gets all yucky and horrible and then you can't eat it and if you do it makes you sick, you know what I mean?

—Ken Robbins

The two biggest sellers in any bookstore are the cookbooks and the diet books. The cookbooks tell you how to prepare the food and the diet books tell you how not to eat any of it.

—Andy Rooney

I used to think...that the English cook the way they do because, through sheer technical deficiency, they had not been able to master the art of cooking. I have discovered to my stupefaction that the English cook that way because that is the way they like it.

—Waverley Root

In the lexicon of lip-smacking, an *epicure* is fastidious in his choice and enjoyment of food, just a soupçon more expert than a *gastronome*; a *gourmet* is a connoisseur of the exotic, taste buds attuned to the calibrations of deliciousness, who savors the masterly techniques of great chefs; a *gourmand* is a hearty bon vivant who enjoys food without truffles and flourishes; a *glutton* overindulges greedily, the word rooted in Latin for "one who devours."...

After eating, an *epicure* gives a thin smile of satisfaction; a *gastronome*, burping into his napkin, praises the food in a magazine; a *gourmet*, repressing his burp, criticizes the food in the same magazine; a *gourmand* belches happily and tells everybody where he ate; a *glutton* embraces the white porcelain altar, or, more plainly, he barfs.

—William Safire

The cook was a good cook, as cooks go; and as cooks go she went.

—Saki (H.H. Munro)

A good cook is like a sorceress who dispenses happiness.

—Elsa Schiaparelli

It is better to be satisfied with probabilities than to demand impossibilities and starve.

—F.C.S. Schiller

How many men are kept busy to humor a single belly!

—Seneca

Appetite, a universal wolf.

—William Shakespeare

There is no love sincerer than the love of food.

—George Bernard Shaw

They all thought she was dead; but my father he kept ladling gin down her throat till she came to so sudden that she bit the bowl off the spoon.

—George Bernard Shaw

You can always tell an old soldier by the inside of his holsters and cartridge boxes. The young ones carry pistols and cartridges; the old ones, grub.

—George Bernard Shaw

When men reach their sixties and retire, they go to pieces. Women go right on cooking.

—Gail Sheehy

All of my experience in the kitchen has taught me that survival depends on letting someone else do the cooking.

—Israel Shenker

On nouvelle cuisine:
The way I feel about it is: Beat me or feed me, but don't tease me. It's toy food; who needs it? Serve it to toy people.
—Jeff Smith (The Frugal Gourmet)

Eat with the rich, but go to play with the poor, who are capable of joy.
—Logan Pearsall Smith

How can they say my life is not a success? Have I not for more than sixty years got enough to eat and escaped being eaten?
—Logan Pearsall Smith

The flavor of social success is delicious, though gravely scorned by those to whose lips the cup has not been proffered.
—Logan Pearsall Smith

I am convinced digestion is the great secret of life.
—Sydney Smith

Life is a difficult thing in the country and it requires a great deal of fore-thought to steer the ship, when you live twelve miles from a lemon.
—Sydney Smith

Hunger finds no fault with the cook.
—C.H. Spurgeon

Promises don't fill the belly.

—C.H. Spurgeon

He is an evil cook that cannot lick his own lips.

—John Stanbridge

THE BOKE OF COKERY

Many of the first publishers were in fact printers. Since they had access to the presses, they often decided what they would turn out. So it was with Rycharde Pynson who in 1500 compiled and published *The Boke of Cokery*—the first cookbook printed in English. Pynson was himself an apprentice under William Caxton, the first printer in Great Britain. Only one copy of the book remains and we can only guess how many copies were printed or sold.

Real happiness comes from inside. Nobody can give it to you. I think I'm happiest when I'm playing with my goddaughter, happiest when I'm riding horses, when I'm with friends, when I'm cooking dinner, when I'm in a darkened audience watching a performer I admire.

—Sharon Stone

My stomach serves me instead of a clock.

—Jonathan Swift

Americans, more than any other culture on earth, are cookbook cooks; we learn to make our meals not from any oral tradition, but from a text. The just-wed cook brings to the new household no carefully copied collection of the family's cherished recipes, but a spanking new edition of *Fannie Farmer* or *The Joy of Cooking*.

—John Thorne

To say that a work of art is good, but incomprehensible to the majority of men, is the same as saying of some kind of food that it is very good but that most people can't eat it.

—Leo Tolstoy

At American weddings, the quality of the food is inversely proportional to the social position of the bride and the groom.

—Calvin Trillin

Don't let love interfere with your appetite. It never does with mine.

—Anthony Trollope

If you can't stand the heat, get out of the kitchen.

—Harry S. Truman

Hunger is the handmaid of genius.
—Mark Twain

Principles have no real force except when one is well fed.

—Mark Twain

To eat is human
To digest divine.
—Mark Twain

Cooking is like love. It should be entered into with abandon or not at all.

—Harriet Van Horne

The feminist movement has helped open minds and kitchens to the notion that men can be at home on the range.

—René Veaux

On the colors of success during his 47-year career at Maxim's:
I started at 18 as a "young *commis*." I wore the traditional white apron then. I graduated to *chef de rang* (tails and white tie), *maître d'hôtel* (tails and black tie), then *assistant-directeur* (dinner jacket) and finally *directeur* (plain business suit—gray at midday, blue at night).

—Roger Viard

Things taste better in small houses.

—Queen Victoria

Occasional examples of bad temper are inevitable in the case of men and women cooks.

—Saint Vincent de Paul

A meal is an artistic social construct, ordering the foodstuffs which comprise it into a complex dramatic whole, as a play organizes actions and words into component parts such as acts, scenes, speeches, dialogues, entrances, and exits, all in the sequences designed for them. However humble it may be, a meal has a definite plot, the intention of which is to intrigue, stimulate, and satisfy.

—Margaret Visser

Happiness is made by the stomach.

—Voltaire

Nothing would be more tiresome than eating and drinking if God had not made them a pleasure as well as a necessity.

—Voltaire

Happy is said to be the family which can eat onions together. They are, for the time being, separate from the world, and have a harmony of aspiration.

—Charles Dudley Warner

I remember that at one time I saw two of my young mistresses and some lady visitors eating ginger cakes, in the yard. At the time those cakes seemed to me to be absolutely the most tempting and desirable things that I have ever seen; and I then and there resolved that, if I ever got free, the height of my ambition would be reached if I could get to the point where I could secure and eat ginger cakes in the way that I saw those ladies doing.

—Booker T. Washington

I've been in more laps than a napkin.
—Mae West

On Chez Panisse, the "citadel of California cuisine" and shaper of American cooking and eating for two decades:
I'm probably the only chef in America who didn't work for Chez Panisse. But I was close enough to know that something was going on, that cooking was changing.

—Jasper White

Cooking is one of those arts which most require to be done by persons of a religious nature.

—Alfred North Whitehead

I hate people who are not serious about their meals.

—Oscar Wilde

There is no sight on earth more appealing than the sight of a woman making dinner for someone she loves.

—Thomas Wolfe

The best cook cannot prepare artistically more than five or six different dishes in one day. A host of mine once had forty courses served at a meal, and as soon as I got home I called for a bowl of rice to still my hunger.

—Yuan Mei